HOT TIPS

FOR

TEACHERS

HOT TIPS

FOR

TEACHERS

30+ STEPS TO STUDENT ENGAGEMENT

Rob Abernathy, M.A., and **Mark Reardon**, M.S.

Skyhouse Publishing

Where to Find Stuff

Dedication

This book is dedicated to our firstborn children, Brooke Danielle Abernathy and Noah Alexander Reardon. Thanks for the joy, inspiration, teachable moments, and memorable stories you bring to our lives daily. We love you!

To Cindy Abernathy, thank you for your careful editing of all my journeys and challenges. Your gentle love and friendship have become a map of support, with generous displays of inspiration, compassion, love, and care.

To Lynn Reardon, thank you for your honesty, your friendship, and your love. You continually demonstrate an unwavering commitment to our relationship and an undying faith in new possibilities.

Acknowledgments

The strategies highlighted in this booklet reflect the brilliance of many teachers and consultants who have dedicated themselves to creating meaningful experiences for students. Thank you for your inspiration and for enhancing our ability to provide educational excellence. We are grateful.

We would like in particular to acknowledge Thomas Armstrong, Suzanne Bailey, Howard Gardner, Merrill Harmin, Madeline Hunter, Eric Jensen, Spencer Kagan, and Learning Forum. We also acknowledge the courageous efforts of the teachers at El Cajon Valley High School Academy and El Capitan High School Academy, Linda Goldstein and the staff at Claire Burgener Academy, Peter Anderson and the staff at Northwood Middle School, and many, many others who make these strategies work on a daily basis.

The implementation of these ideas is enthusiastically encouraged!

Thank you!

Introduction

We wrote this book to provide educators with field-tested strategies for increasing student engagement. By engagement we mean students' interaction with the curriculum and their participation in class. In this day of standards-based curricula and heightened teacher accountability, improving student engagement is the way to produce measurable improvements in student achievement. We believe it is possible to improve students' performance by improving the way we teach and the way students learn. Enjoy making these strategies come alive in your classroom!

What Are HotTips?

HotTips are a collection of strategies that have worked for us, have worked for our friends, and will work for you. In this book you will find valuable techniques and strategies for motivating students, improving their retention, and fostering a sense of excitement about learning. These tips get results.

Most tips are our original ideas, a few are borrowed, and others are modified. Each HotTip has been tested and used with students in a variety of settings and grade levels. They add value to the planning and delivery of your lessons. We offer these HotTips as tools. We hope they will validate and enhance what you already do effectively.

You will find that several of the HotTips are related. For example, Preview Coming Attractions, Leave Open Loops, and Create Infomercials are all ways to introduce upcoming content in a manner that builds students' interest and motivation to learn. Similarly, Pop the Quickie Quiz and Collect a Ticket out the Door are both strategies for holding students accountable for the material you presented in a lesson. Obviously, you would not use redundant strategies in the same lesson. But variety is the spice of life—and the condiment for learning. When your lessons fall into a routine, the students' brains will soon shut down and turn off.

We suggest you read through all the HotTips. Try them all, then take the ones that work best for you and integrate them into your own toolkit of great ideas. Periodically shake up your delivery and keep engagement high by trying a new HotTip or putting a different spin on a familiar HotTip.

What Is a HotTips Book?

A HotTips book is

> ➤ an effective tool that makes learning and information come alive through interactive text and activities
> ➤ an artfully designed workbook with space for you to record your thoughts, writings, drawings, and personal interaction
> ➤ an information-to-knowledge-to-application tool that provides relevant, brain-friendly, and immediately applicable strategies
> ➤ a collection of innovative and foundational information that will enhance your effectiveness in the classroom

This HotTips book will enhance your skill integration and implementation. It will amplify your natural abilities by helping you tap into your knowledge, experience, and creativity while capitalizing on brain-compatible learning strategies. The activities take you beyond information to integration and application. As you work with the design, you will experience how it becomes smart, relevant, and useful. The more actively you engage yourself with the activities and applications, the more valuable this book becomes.

Look for more books in the HotTips series. *HotTips for Speakers: 25 Surefire Ways to Engage and Captivate Any Group or Audience* contains valuable techniques and strategies for public speaking, presenting, teaching, training, and facilitating. Also look for HotTips specifically geared to group facilitation.

Imagine This

You have been invited to represent teachers of the United States of America as a specialist in instructional and pedagogical strategies to increase student engagement. You are a successful teacher, have been recognized by your peers as an innovative leader on the topic, and will be flown (first class) to an educational summit to be united with an international group of teachers who are also experts at increasing student engagement.

At the first gathering, you are presented with a collective challenge to create the Top 10 List of Sure-Fire Strategies to Increase Student Engagement. Collectively you are to create the top 10 list of strategies that you use or have used, have seen used, or have heard about through your best practices network. What might you and your expert colleagues suggest as the Top 10 Sure-Fire Strategies to Increase Student Engagement?

Using your own ideas, the ideas of mentors, innovative educators you have learned from, and the voices of "best practice" (which represents the international group of teachers), create your own top 10 list.

Top 10 List of Sure-Fire Strategies to Increase Student Engagement

1. _____

2. _____

3. _____

4. _____

5. _____

6. _____

7. _____

8. _____

9. _____

10. _____

How Is This HotTips Book Organized?

Pages 5 and 6 preview the layout of this HotTips book and how you will use it. Each HotTip follows the same format, with icons to guide you to specific information. So grab a colored pen or pencil, or perhaps a highlighter. Leave your fingerprints on these pages through your pictures, symbols, words, color, and reflective thoughts. Then feel the impact of each HotTip tomorrow in your classroom.

Each chapter title is the name of a HotTip. We have attempted to group the tips logically, with sections for the opening, middle, and closing of a lesson and related HotTips grouped together.

The HotTip is defined in an action phrase that distills its essence in easily remembered language.

Between the quotation marks is an affirmation designed to strengthen your internal beliefs. Say this thought often.

Making It Mine is designed specifically to guide implementation. It contains brain-compatible learning strategies that help you cement the HotTip into your repertoire. This section will take you well on your way toward mastery!

Use Reach for the Stars as an iconic bar graph to chart your mastery of the HotTip! Mark or circle the appropriate stars to monitor stages of your development with this HotTip. The lower star represents initial implementation, the middle star a feeling of progress, and the top star competence. Three stars mean you are on top of this HotTip!

Distill the meaning of this HotTip for you by imagining what you would say if you were explaining its importance to a coworker. Or, if you prefer, draw an icon that represents the meaning of the HotTip for you.

Thinking It Over provides a place to reflect on what you have learned. If you are too busy to reflect, you are too busy to grow. Think about it!

Making This Book Mine

Do I . . .?

How Do I . . . ?

Why Do I . . . ?

These three simple questions contain powerful reflective value that deepens and accelerates your learning. They affect your future success with tools and strategies to increase student engagement. We invite you to "go meta" and, with the positive intent to grow and deepen your skills as a professional educator, to think about your teaching practice from a reflective state. Go beyond what you have previously reflected or thought about in your teaching. No matter what stage you are at in your teaching journey, it is always valuable to pause, reflect, and have a courageous conversation with yourself. So go ahead, ponder this activity and respond to the questions on page 8.

Do I engage and support all students in my learning environment?

How Do I engage and support all students in my learning environment?

Why Do I engage and support all students in my learning environment?

When you take the time to engage in thought and reflection, you strengthen your effectiveness as a teacher. Asking the three preceding questions helps you:

- ➤ reflect about student learning, student engagement, and teaching practice
- ➤ formulate professional goals to improve teaching practice
- ➤ guide, monitor, and assess the progress of your teaching practice
- ➤ move you toward professional goals and professionally accepted benchmarks of success

For each of the questions on page 8, prompt your best thinking by asking yourself, *"Do I . . . ?" "How Do I . . . ? "* or *"Why Do I . . . ?"*

As a teacher, do I draw on students' prior knowledge, helping them to see the connections between what they already know and the new material? How and why do I do so?

_____

_____

_____

As a teacher, do I use a variety of instructional strategies and resources to respond to students' diverse needs? How and why do I do so?

_____

_____

_____

As a teacher, do I facilitate learning experiences that provide opportunities for independent and collaborative learning? How and why do I do so?

_____

_____

_____

As a teacher, do I engage students in problem solving, critical thinking, and other activities that make subject matter meaningful? How and why do I do so?

_____

_____

_____

As a teacher, do I promote self-directed, reflective learning for all students? How and why do I do so?

_____

_____

_____

Now, take this reflective state with you as you read the HotTips in this book. It's time to begin!

HotTips for Teachers ©2002 Zephyr Press, Chicago, IL • (800) 232-2187 • www.zephyrpress.com

Part 1

HotTips for Opening the Lesson

Student engagement happens in a myriad of ways. Catching students' attention at the start of the day or lesson makes it easier to keep them tuned in for the rest of the time. You have several options for creating an atmosphere of purposeful engagement from the very beginning so every student learns in every lesson, every day. You may choose to captivate them from the moment they see your doorway (Draw the Learning Line) or during the opening moments of the class or day (Ask Opening Questions, Flash Review-Preview Cards). You can also entice them through the room setup (Fill Your Room with I.D. Posters, Envision Engaging Environments, Get Visual) and in the way you introduce your class (Create Infomercials, Preview Coming Attractions).

Draw the
Learning Line

Make a brightly colored "learning line" at the doorway to remind everyone entering the classroom to bring a positive attitude toward learning and each other.

One great benefit of being human is the ability to choose. We have choices about most of the events in our lives: what we wear, what we eat, what we drive, who we hang around with, and how we spend our time. Our ability to choose extends to how we feel, what we think, and how we act. We can even choose our attitude at any given moment.

Given this truth, here's an interesting question: What would your classroom be like if students arrived with a willing attitude, ready to participate and learn? Could you accomplish more? Use your time more productively? Reteach less? Most likely! So let's create such an environment. Let's capitalize on the human ability to choose in order to create an atmosphere where learning and learners are supported and nurtured.

Have a conversation with your students. Ask them, "What makes for a class from which everyone can benefit?" Record their responses on the chalkboard or chart paper. Feel free to add your ideas as well. If the students don't mention "attitude" or "frame of mind," suggest these and add them to the list.

You might remind students that everyone in class has the right to learn, and that each person's mood, frame of mind, or attitude (yours included) affects the whole class's ability to learn well. (You may want to use the first paragraph of this HotTip to point out how easy and natural it is to make choices.)

Now suggest the idea of a "learning line"—a line drawn on the floor at the doorway that reminds each person who enters to choose a willing, cooperative, respectful attitude. Role-play crossing the line and transforming your attitude from one of lethargy and grumpiness to one of possibility, interest, and empathy. Let students know that you understand they have a life outside your class—family, extracurricular activities, jobs, and friends—and that bad things can happen in life, affecting their attitude. The learning line is not meant to discount those events and experiences, but it is meant to remind everyone—the teacher included—how our attitude influences our ability to learn.

 The learning line reminds me and my students that we can choose to be ready to learn.

Making It Mine

After you and your students have talked about the power of choice and have agreed to make this concept work to your advantage, paint a colorful line at the threshold of your classroom door (or use colored tape). Stencil "Learning Line" on it. Make the line cheerful and fun, and watch how it changes even your attitude!

Reach for the Stars! ✩ ✩ ★ ✦ ★

Use the stars below to monitor your progress.

I have this tip
down cold!

It is familiar
territory.

This tip feels like a
new pair of shoes.

If a colleague asked you about Draw the Learning Line, what would you say? Write your answer here, or if you prefer, draw an icon that represents this HotTip.

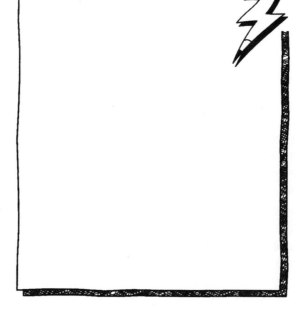

Thinking It Over

How has Draw the Learning Line affected
students' attitudes, and how can I tell?

_____

_____

_____

_____

_____

_____

What will I do differently next time?

_____

_____

_____

_____

When I cross the learning line, I am reminded that students . . .

_____

_____

_____

_____

What do my students say about Draw the Learning Line?

_____

_____

_____

_____

On a scale of 1 to 10, my students give Draw the Learning Line a

_____.

Fill Your Room
with I.D. Posters

Hang posters at eye level with affirmations about students' abilities and the content you are teaching.

Do you have a voice inside your head? Yes, I mean the one that just said, "Are you talking to me?" We all have a little voice that talks to us when we are in new and challenging situations. Depending on our past experiences, our internal voice might be encouraging ("I can do it!" "I can make it!" "That's it, keep going!") or discouraging ("You want me to do *what?*" "I've never been any good at that.") We refer to this voice as our I.D., or internal dialogue. The voices inside our heads—and the ones inside our students' heads—are the most powerful determinant of learning success. Think about it. This claim makes sense, doesn't it? What we say to ourselves powerfully influences our ability.

Are there ways to cultivate positive internal dialogue in your students, a voice that would propel them forward rather than hold them back? Of course there are! One strategy is to have students say positive sentences aloud. For example, "I can learn this!" "This is getting easier for me!" "I am smart and gifted!" Also have students say positive statements to one another. Here are a few examples: "You can do it!" "Hey, I'll bet you've always been really smart." "Way to go! Great problem solving!"

I.D. posters are one more way to influence and shape the voice inside students' heads. Create 11" x 17" posters with affirming statements you want students to say to themselves: statements about their abilities, the content they are learning, and the goals for the classroom. Examples include:

Am I **Learning** or what!	I'm getting **Smarter** with every new challenge!	**Math Matters** . . . and I can prove it!

Place the posters so they are at eye level when students are seated. As students glance around the room, they read messages that strengthen the positive attitudes and thoughts they need for success.

I can influence my students'—and my own—internal dialogue.

Making It Mine

What would you like your students to say about learning, about your content, or about themselves? Create two I.D. posters. Better yet, have the students collaborate to create posters with the content you specify. Remember to make the most important words in the statement colorful and bold. Every few weeks rotate the posters or put up a new set to keep interest.

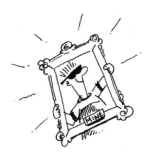

Reach for the Stars!

Use the stars below to monitor your progress.

I have this tip
down cold!

It is familiar
territory.

This tip feels like a
new pair of shoes.

If a student teacher asked you about Fill Your Room with I.D. Posters, what would you say? Write your answer here, or if you prefer, draw an icon that represents this HotTip.

HotTips for Teachers ©2002 Zephyr Press, Chicago, IL • (800) 232-2187 • www.zephyrpress.com

Thinking It Over

What other I.D. posters could I make?
(Sketch them here.)

 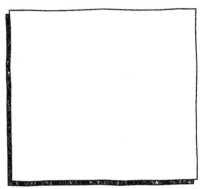

What's the biggest challenge I face in Filling My Room with I.D. Posters?

_____

_____

How will I solve this challenge?

_____

_____

When I Fill My Room with I.D. Posters, I am reminded that students . . .

_____

_____

How do my students react to the I.D. Posters?

_____

_____

On a scale of 1 to 10, my students give Fill Your Room with I.D. Posters a _____.

Ask Opening Questions

Establish an opening ritual of repeating a set of questions and answers about the goals of the class at the beginning of each day or period.

Getting students focused at the beginning of class can be challenging. Ask Opening Questions creates a tradition that reminds students of their purpose together and builds a sense of belonging. Here is how this HotTip works:

1. Consider the purpose or main goals of your class: To learn? To gain skills necessary to get into college? To think like a mathematician? To develop social skills? To become better writers? To explore new possibilities?

2. Develop three or four questions the answers to which reflect these goals. Then choose a succinct, easy-to-remember answer for each one. For example:

Question	Answer
Why are we here?	To learn
What will we give today?	Our very best
What will we get from today?	Everything we can
What matters?	Math matters
How smart are we?	Very smart
Where are we headed?	The colleges of our choice

3. Students arrive and get settled in. On your cue or at the sound of the bell, everyone stands. Either you or (better yet) a student stands at the front of the room and recites each question in turn as the class responds in unison. "Why are we here?" "To learn!" "What matters?" "Math matters!" and so on.

4. Encourage the class to speak in unison with gusto and to stand tall.

5. While the class engages in the opening questions, you can take attendance or do any last-minute preparations for the fabulous lesson you are about to teach. Like other opening rituals, Ask Opening Questions helps students focus while emphasizing the class goals. This ritual sets the tone and sends a message: In here we participate and stay on track.

 I increase focus, participation, and sense of purpose by Asking Opening Questions.

Making It Mine

Take a moment to write the purpose and goals of your class. Next, develop the leading questions and the corresponding answers.

Purpose and goals:

_____

_____

_____

Question	**Answer**
_____	_____
_____	_____
_____	_____

For the debut of Ask Opening Questions, write the questions and answers on an overhead or the chalkboard so everyone can learn them. You may need to coach the student leader to ask the questions with vigor and confidence. Likewise, coach the class regarding their participation, the volume of their responses, and the purpose behind opening questions.

Reach for the Stars!

Use the stars below to monitor your progress.

I have this tip down cold!

It is familiar territory.

This tip feels like a new pair of shoes.

If a student teacher asked why you Ask Opening Questions, what would you say? Write your answer here, or if you prefer, draw an icon that represents this HotTip.

Thinking It Over

How has Ask Opening Questions affected
students' attitudes, and how can I tell?

_____

_____

_____

_____

_____

_____

Are there any opening questions I want to modify or replace?

_____

_____

_____

_____

When I Ask Opening Questions, I am reminded that students . . .

_____

_____

_____

_____

What do my students say about Ask Opening Questions?

_____

_____

_____

_____

On a scale of 1 to 10, my students give Ask Opening Questions a

_____.

Flash Review–
Preview Cards

Have the class respond in unison to giant flash cards summarizing the preceding lesson and previewing the next.

Have you noticed that students treat every day in class as a completely new day—to the point of not even remembering what they learned the day before? We call it the "BTDT syndrome" (been there, done that). We believe part of the problem is that students perceive school as a disjointed parade of unrelated, irrelevant knowledge and facts. We teachers do not see it this way, but many students do.

An opening ritual that vaccinates against the BTDT syndrome and helps focus your students is Flash Review-Preview Cards. Think of these cards as large flash cards with words, statements, or questions on one side and answers on the other. They work like this: A student leader stands at the front of the room holding each review-preview card above his or her head. Standing and speaking in unison, the class reads the cards, supplying any missing information. After the class responds, the leader turns the card over long enough for everyone to see the answer, then moves to the next card.

Some cards might contain a key word or phrase, such as "legislative" or "three branches of government," which the class is simply to read. Other cards might be in fill-in-the-blank form, such as "checks and _____." In unison the students fill in the blank with "balances." Some cards might contain a question, such as, "What form of government do we have?" After reading the card, students respond with the answer, "representative democracy." Review-preview cards could even contain icons (see "Get Visual," p. 26), to which students would respond with the idea the icon represents—for example, the formula for the area of a geometric shape. Still other cards may have information from an upcoming portion of the unit or next chapter—for example, "monarchy." By stacking the deck with a few concepts yet to be studied, you start your students' minds on a meaning-making journey: They attempt to make sense of the new concepts in the context of what they already know. During the review-preview session, listen to their responses in order to identify concepts about which they are still confused.

 I help my students learn, recall, and transfer information by Flashing Review-Preview Cards.

Making It Mine

First, make a list of the key words, concepts, diagrams, or formulas for the unit you are currently teaching. Consider whether the concept is best presented as a word, phrase, fill-in-the-blank phrase, or question. Place each on a separate card. If the card contains a blank or a question, write the answer on the back.

Concept	Format for Presentation
_____	_____
_____	_____
_____	_____
_____	_____

Introduce the cards by asking how many students would like to get better grades or to remember the information they have learned more easily. Explain that the review-preview cards will help them put information into their long-term memory banks.

Reach for the Stars!

Use the stars below to monitor your progress.

I have this tip
down cold!

It is familiar
territory.

This tip feels like a
new pair of shoes.

If the PTA president asked you about Flash Review-Preview Cards, what would you say? Write your answer here, or if you prefer, draw an icon that represents this HotTip.

HotTips for Teachers ©2002 Zephyr Press, Chicago, IL • (800) 232-2187 • www.zephyrpress.com

Thinking It Over

What difference has Flash Review-Preview Cards made to students' learning, and how can I tell?

_____

_____

_____

_____

What will I do differently next time?

_____

_____

_____

_____

When I Flash Review-Preview Cards, I am reminded that students . . .

_____

_____

_____

_____

Which cards did my students master most quickly? Why?

Card	**Reason**
_____	_____
_____	_____
_____	_____
_____	_____

On a scale of 1 to 10, my students give Flash Review-Preview Cards a _____.

Get Visual

Use icons and graphic organizers to help students visualize information.

M ore than 90 percent of the information that comes to our brains is visual, and our eyes can register 36,000 visual messages per hour (Jensen 1994). Yet much of our instruction is auditory. We use phrases like, "Listen to me." "Did you hear me?" "Does that sound right to you?" "Tell me your answer." Undoubtedly, these auditory cues are useful and indeed necessary, but strengthening them with visual cues amplifies students' ability to encode and retrieve information quickly. In an age of information saturation, visual cues are extremely useful. They help us to make sense of information by displaying how things are related. The visual parts of the brain like to see the big picture, to see how everything fits together. Let's take a look at three Get Visual strategies: iconic posters, visual language, and graphic organizers.

Iconic Posters

An iconic poster is a symbolic representation of key concepts or steps in your content (DePorter, Singer-Nourie, and Reardon 1999). Drawn in color on a large sheet of construction paper, this picture serves two purposes:

1. It creates an image in students' minds. Since the mind encodes information in metaphoric-symbolic language, iconic posters speak the language of the brain.

2. It creates a sense of curiosity and anticipation. Even before they know what the icons mean, students begin trying to

decode the meaning of them. The poster to the right is an example of an iconic poster for the three primary learning modalities (visual, auditory, and kinesthetic).

Visual Language

Visual language is the careful use of words and phrases to cue the visual domain of learning. For example: "This will clear it up for you." "Picture yourself as a carbon molecule." "Look closely at the diagram." "See what I mean?" "Imagine this. . . . " Findings from neurolinguistics, the study of how language is encoded and processed in the brain, suggest that using words with visual content helps students access the visual modality (Bandler 1985).

Graphic Organizers

Graphic organizers are visual representations that help the brain see connections and relationships among pieces of information. Examples are Mind Maps, webs, concept maps, and flowcharts.

 I help my students retain and recall information each time I Get Visual.

Making It Mine

Sketch out an iconic poster and a graphic organizer in the boxes provided.

Reach for the Stars!

Use the stars below to monitor your progress.

I have this tip
down cold!

It is familiar
territory.

This tip feels like a
new pair of shoes.

If a colleague asked you about Get Visual, what would you say?
Write your answer here, or if you prefer, draw an icon that
represents this HotTip.

HotTips for Teachers ©2002 Zephyr Press, Chicago, IL • (800) 232-2187 • www.zephyrpress.com

Thinking It Over

What other iconic posters or graphic organizers could I make? (Sketch them here.)

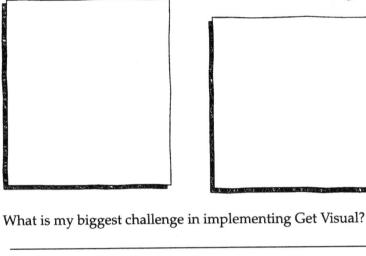

What is my biggest challenge in implementing Get Visual?

_____

_____

How can I solve this challenge?

_____

_____

When I use iconic posters or graphic organizers, I am reminded that my students . . .

_____

_____

What have my students noticed about Get Visual?

_____

_____

_____

On a scale of 1 to 10, my students give Get Visual a _____.

Create Infomercials

Present to students the benefits of your class or lesson.

In marketing, an infomercial is a description of the benefits, value, and features of a particular product. It highlights what the customer gains by buying the product. It succinctly yet descriptively captures the essence of the product while detailing the most salient points.

What is *your* product? It is both the *content* (knowledge) and the *process* (skills) of your class. Not only do students become more knowledgeable, they also become more intelligent. For example, the content of your class might be algebra or English, and your objective that students will understand the FOIL method or the Schaeffer writing process. Thereby they will increase their skills (process): the ability to unravel a mathematical problem or organize their thoughts into a logical sequence.

Crafting an infomercial is simple. Here is how to do it:

1. Make a list of the most salient, interesting, or necessary facts and information about your class or lesson.
2. Make a list of the important skills addressed: creativity, problem solving, extemporaneous speaking, organization, and so on.
3. Answer the following questions to pinpoint the value of the lesson:

- Why would students want to be here?
- What benefit or value will they get?
- What are the unique features, benchmarks, or milestones?
- What have others said about the benefits that might serve as a testimonial?

4. Consider a metaphor that best describes what this lesson will be like: an adventure, a safari, a roller coaster, a voyage, house construction, a concert, or whatever.

5. Consider what life will be like for your students when they successfully complete this event. Paint a picture of their future selves. Tell them what they will be able to know and do because they did well.

Presenting your infomercial can be fun. Here are the steps:

Demonstrations/enrolling questions: Begin with a demonstration or a set of enrolling questions. (Enrolling questions usually begin with "How many of you . . ." or "Raise your hand if . . ."). Capture students' attention by tapping into their prior experience or knowledge. The demonstration might take the form of reading a "before and after" essay (English), presenting a slide show of interesting places (geography), or solving the gnarliest problem they will encounter right before their very eyes (math).

Future status: Reveal what life will be like for students when they successfully complete your course or lesson.

Success criteria: Share with students how the rosy future you just painted can be theirs. For example, "People just like you who remember to communicate with me, collaborate with each other, do their best each day, and be respectful to others do really well here." In addition to giving your set of success criteria, elicit from students what they think is required in order to complete this class with pride.

Above all, speak with leadership, passion, and a sense of common purpose. You are all in this together!

With each infomercial I create, my students more clearly under-stand my expectations.

Making It Mine

Using the steps provided in the introductory section, design an infomercial for your course or lesson. Remember to build a bridge between students' current abilities, knowledge, and beliefs and the course outcomes. Fully describe the value and benefits, as well as the challenges ahead and what it will take to be successful.

Demonstrations/enrolling questions: _____

_____

Future status: _____

_____

Success criteria: _____

_____

Reach for the Stars! ⭐⭐⭐⭐⭐

Use the stars below to monitor your progress.

I have this tip down cold!

It is familiar territory.

This tip feels like a new pair of shoes.

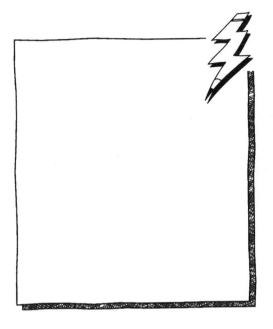

If a student asked you about Create Info-mercials, what would you say? Write your answer here, or if you prefer, draw an icon that represents this HotTip.

Thinking It Over

Did my students "buy in" to my lesson more when I used the Create Infomercials technique? If they did, how do I know? If they didn't, what specifically about the technique needs to be changed?

_____

_____

_____

_____

In what other ways, or during what other times, could I (or my students) Create Infomercials?

_____

_____

_____

_____

Preview Coming Attractions

Present your learning objectives in a form that creates an air of mystery and curiosity.

Previews accomplish two things:

1. They provide an initial, broad overview of a lesson.
2. They stimulate interest by suggesting there is "more than meets the eye."

Movies at the theater or on video are always preceded by previews of forthcoming features. Viewers sit mesmerized by the montage of scenes and sound bites. Even the local late-night newscaster leads us to believe that the "late-breaking" story is worth staying up for! Previews have a profound ability to create interest. They give us just enough to tease our taste buds, touch our hearts, or tweak our minds—and they keep us coming back!

How could you apply this strategy in your classroom? Rather than writing the objective or standard on the board so that students can predetermine their participation level, try "disguising it" to create interest. For example: "Making others believe your ideas: Persuasion and what it doesn't want you to know" (persuasive essays). "If you only knew, you'd live there too!" (geography).

Imagine that your students are about to learn the Pythagorean theorem ($a^2 + b^2 = c^2$). If you say, "Tomorrow we'll learn to find the hypotenuse of a right triangle with the Pythagorean theorem," students might feel less than enthusiastic about returning. So, how could you introduce the topic differently, in a way that piques their interest? How about: "Tomorrow you'll want to be here, and not just here but in the best seat possible. Because tomorrow we'll spend the day solving puzzles, much the way Indiana Jones or Sherlock Holmes did." Or write on the board: "Tomorrow: What you and Indiana Jones have in common." Previews build curiosity and provide a big-picture enticement for coming attractions.

 Preview Coming Attractions helps me create anticipation for and interest in an upcoming lesson.

Making It Mine

Study how the movie industry, tabloids, and television talk shows capture your attention. Listen for the language used in previews. Listen to the tone and pace of the announcer's voice. Then take tomorrow's objective and turn it into an attention-getting, interest-grabbing preview.

Warning: Creating previews may be habit forming. Side effects include piqued curiosity and intense interest. Use only in the company of students.

Reach for the Stars! ★ ★ ★ ✦ ✦

Use the stars below to monitor your progress.

I have this tip
down cold!

It is familiar
territory.

This tip feels like a
new pair of shoes.

If a friend asked you about Preview Coming Attractions, what would you say? Write your answer here, or if you prefer, draw an icon that represents this HotTip.

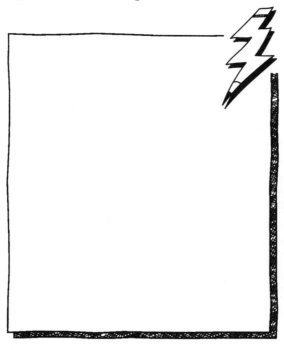

Thinking It Over

What worked well, and how do I know
it worked?

_____

_____

_____

_____

_____

What will I do differently next time?

_____

_____

_____

_____

When I Preview Coming Attractions, I am reminded that students . . .

_____

_____

_____

_____

What have my students noticed about my use of Preview Coming
Attractions?

_____

_____

_____

_____

On a scale of 1 to 10, my students give Preview Coming Attractions
a _____.

Envision Engaging Environments

Establish learning areas in your classroom that encourage students to engage themselves with the content in a wide variety of ways.

Consider this claim: There are an infinite number of intelligences, an infinite number of ways for people to be smart (Armstrong 1993, 8–9; see also Gardner 1993). Yet from IQ scores to stanines, from modality preferences to learning styles, from personalities to the theory of multiple intelligences, we continue to teach to one, two, or at best three of the intelligences. The theory of multiple intelligences offers us a greater variety of teaching tools (Gardner 1993; Lazear 2000; Armstrong 1993): visual-spatial, linguistic, interpersonal, musical, naturalist, bodily-kinesthetic, intrapersonal, and logical-mathematical.

We are offering a radical new frame for designing and creating intelligent space in your classroom learning environment. Consider this: Each of the eight intelligences can be explored in a multiplicity of ways. Or, to conceptualize the idea another way: All of the millions of hues we see every day are derived from the seven spectral colors of the rainbow.

How could your classroom environment tap into a variety of your students' intelligences? How could your learning space elicit and stimulate all the myriad of ways your students are smart? Explore your answers to these questions as you build an environment rich with possibility.

 I can accelerate my students' learning by creating multiple ways to interact with the learning environment.

Making It Mine

Imagine a variety of learning areas in your classroom where students could explore content in a variety of ways. Allow the ideas that follow to spark your imagination, your creativity, and your lesson design.

NATURALIST

Aquarium: Students learn about different underwater species and their peculiarities.

Observation Station: Here students will find a variety of observational tools: binoculars, microscopes, cameras, and magnifying glasses, as well as natural items to observe.

VISUAL-SPATIAL

Artist's Pad: Students work on paintings, drawings, sculptures.

Image Gallery: Students look through old magazines to find pictures and text for projects.

Cyber Artists: Students interact with computer graphics, paint programs, and 3D rendering software.

Drafting Tables: Students draft blueprints and build models in an area containing drawing and drafting supplies.

VERBAL-LINGUISTIC

Library Zone: Students explore an in-class library filled with the works.

Crash Pad: Students read while lounging on beanbags, pillows, and chairs.

The Dialogue Den: This popular student hangout is a place to have quiet chats with partners about teacher-planned or student-generated questions, plan team projects, and discuss important issues.

Quiet Writers: Abundant supplies of writing materials, as well as computers loaded with word-processing software, are present in this quiet area of the classroom where students can go to write.

INTERPERSONAL

The Coffee House: Students can chat without disturbing others in this cozy corner. Comfortable furniture encourages students to sit facing each other and interact socially.

Game Space: This table and floor space is where students can play a variety of games together.

Tutoring Table: Students assist one another on class work, projects, and extension activities.

LOGICAL-MATHEMATICAL

Think Tank: Students solve problems and strengthen their critical or creative thinking. In this space students will find cards with challenging problems to solve, brain teasers, and logic puzzles.

Mad Scientists' Lab: Students put on their lab coats and find an array of hands-on materials to explore. They lead themselves through step-by-step science experiments.

MUSICAL

Recording Studio: Students record their projects and musical renderings in a "production studio" containing tape recorders, mixers, video tape, digital cameras, and computer technologies. Listening centers are set up for private listening.

Cyber Soundstage: In this area, students compose futuristic sounds, play with the classics, tinker with sound effects, and create original songs with the aid of the computer.

INTRAPERSONAL

Kokomo: This is an intimate, topically focused, private spot where students can go to be alone for a while. In this space they might find a lounge chair, headphones with music, cool drinking water, and posters with tropical themes.

Concentration Station: Here is another private spot where students can go to be alone with their work and their thoughts. This spot is strategically located to be distraction-free. Earplugs and cubicles are possible additions.

BODILY-KINESTHETIC

The Theatre: Students go to this closet filled with costumes and props to rehearse plays or skits they make up.

Workshop: Students assemble various projects and tinker with an assortment of tools, building materials, old appliances, and electrical gadgets.

Dance Floor: Here students learn dances of different times and cultures. They can create their own expressive dance movements and other choreographed expressions.

Reach for the Stars!

Use the stars below to monitor your progress.

**I have this tip
down cold!**

**It is familiar
territory.**

**This tip feels like a
new pair of shoes.**

If your principal asked you about Envision Engaging Environments, what would you say? Write your answer here, or if you prefer, draw an icon that represents this HotTip.

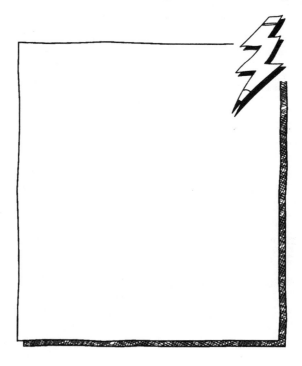

HotTips for Teachers ©2002 Zephyr Press, Chicago, IL • (800) 232-2187 • www.zephyrpress.com

Thinking It Over

What worked well, and how do I know
it worked?

_____

_____

_____

_____

_____

How will I extend this idea with future learning areas?

_____

_____

_____

_____

When I Envision Engaging Environments, I am reminded that
students . . .

_____

_____

_____

_____

How have my students responded to my use of Envision Engaging
Environments?

_____

_____

_____

_____

On a scale of 1 to 10, my students give Envision Engaging
Environments a _____.

Part 2

HotTips for Conducting the Lesson

The familiar adage, "Now you see it. Now you don't" all too often describes students' participation as the lesson progresses or the year continues. How many times have you said to yourself, "I had them at the beginning, but something happened along the way"? This phenomenon can occur even during some of your best lessons. This section contains antidotes to the doldrums. Watch how your students perk up when you Speak to the Best Self, Reach Inside, Pick up the Pace, Regain Focus with Diffusers, and Interject State Changers. You can continue to pique their curiosity when you Dramatize Your Point, Put the Content in Motion, and Leave Open Loops. Your students will really start participating when they Listen-Write, Synthesize Learning with KnowBooks, and learn cooperatively (Bring Me Your Brains, Draw on Guided Peer Teaching). To ensure students are following the lesson, Make Call Backs and Elicit Thinking, then Ask for Classwide Signaling or have students Box Their Understanding. Go ahead, Celebrate Success and Engage Your Heart to create a positive environment in your classroom. Your students will want to be present in class, in the front row, every day.

Speak to the Best Self

Phrase your expectations for behavior and accomplishment in positive terms that call on students' best qualities.

Like any teacher, no doubt you have experienced times when students exhibited inappropriate behavior or turned in assignments that did not meet your expectations. How do you encourage students to give you appropriate behavior and the quality of work you want? Speak to their best selves! Tap into the best qualities resident inside them—commitment, attentiveness, respect, kindness, diligence, trustworthiness, and patience. Call on those qualities and challenge students to rise to the occasion!

Here is what Speak to the Best Self might sound like when you are addressing the class:

> We've been writing our paragraphs about plants, and we've made a nice start. As we complete them today, stick with it. Use your ability to analyze. Find the words and sentences that aren't quite right—the ones that need more detail. Take a closer look at what you truly want to say and choose the best word or words to say it. Let these paragraphs be your best work.

To an individual student, speak privately so as neither to embarrass the child unnecessarily nor to provide an audience for misbehavior:

Mark, what I'm noticing in class today is different than what I've seen from you in the past. You've been interrupting people while they are talking and while they are doing their work. Is something bothering you today? (Pause for the student to respond, then continue.) Most of the time you are respectful and considerate of others. Can you find that part of you today and let it shine? Thanks.

This strategy maintains rapport with students while re-establishing your expectations. By calling on their better qualities, you send the message that you believe they are capable of showing those aspects of themselves. It also sends the message that although your expectations are high, they are attainable. Speaking to the best self is a powerful reminder that we all have choices. We constantly choose how we will act and what we will say. Often students simply need a reminder that they can make better choices—choices that better reflect who they truly are.

 When I Speak to the Best Self, I remind students how capable they truly are.

Making It Mine

Think of your next lesson or project. Make a list of qualities that students will need to exhibit in order to do their very best. These qualities might include focus, persistence, creativity, risk-taking, or organization. Consider how you might present these expectations in a positive way. Get ready to watch students rise to the occasion!

Qualities: _____

_____

How to present: _____

_____

Reach for the Stars!

Use the stars below to monitor your progress.

I have this tip
down cold!

It is familiar
territory.

This tip feels like a
new pair of shoes.

If one of your students asked you why you Speak to the Best Self, what would you say? Write your answer here, or if you prefer, draw an icon that represents this HotTip.

Thinking It Over

What worked well, and how do I know
it worked?

_____

_____

_____

_____

_____

What will I do differently next time?

_____

_____

_____

_____

When I Speak to the Best Self, I am reminded that students . . .

_____

_____

_____

_____

How do my students respond when I Speak to the Best Self?

_____

_____

_____

_____

On a scale of 1 to 10, my students give Speak to the Best Self a

_____.

Reach Inside

Address students' internal dialogue by commenting on what they may be saying to themselves about a lesson or task.

Have you ever noticed that some students look down when they don't know the answer to a question? (Do they think we can't see them?) Do your students seem amazed that you know what they are thinking?

The internal world of students is full of emotions, opinions, and preconceived ideas about life and learning—more specifically about school, about you, or about your content area: "I hate math," "English is hard," "I can't draw," "School is boring," are a few examples of students' internal dialogues. As you can imagine, those thoughts and feelings can hinder their performance.

Addressing what students say inside their heads takes their invisible internal world and makes it visible, helping them to stay focused. By anticipating students' problematic thoughts and reactions to your content, you can design lessons based on rapport and understanding. Here are a few examples of how you might Reach Inside your students' heads:

- ➤ "You might be thinking, 'This isn't very important.' I used to think that, too."

- ➤ "You might be wondering, 'What does this have to do with anything?' Have you considered . . . ?"

- ➤ "You might be asking yourself, 'Is this the fastest way to solve this problem?' Brilliant question. This isn't even close to the fastest way, but it's the most accurate."

- ➤ "You may have just said, 'Wow! This is going to be a bunch of work!' And it will be if you wait until the last minute. We'll do this project in sections."

- ➤ "Have you ever thought, 'This is a waste of my time'? Well, it's a waste of time only if it takes longer than it needs to!"

You may also want to try these variations on the theme of Reach Inside. Reach Inside their hearts with a statement like, "You might be feeling, 'Wow! This all feels a bit overwhelming.'" Or Reach Inside their lives with comments like, "This is just like being at the mall." "Skateboarding involves a similar mathematical principle."

 I build rapport and understanding when I Reach Inside my students.

Making It Mine

You might be wondering, "When do I use this Reach Inside strategy?" Great question. Use it when you know students will react to what you are teaching or the activity you are about to do. Also look into the faces of your students often as you move through the lesson. You will notice visible clues that reveal their internal dialogues.

Take a moment to think like your students about an upcoming lesson or activity. Make a list of the two or three thoughts they are most likely to have. As you rehearse the lesson, anticipate when most students might be entertaining those thoughts, then Reach Inside!

Reach for the Stars!

Use the stars below to monitor your progress.

**I have this tip
down cold!**

**It is familiar
territory.**

**This tip feels like a
new pair of shoes.**

If a colleague asked you about Reach Inside, what would you say?
Write your answer here, or if you prefer, draw an icon that
represents this HotTip.

HotTips for Teachers ©2002 Zephyr Press, Chicago, IL • (800) 232-2187 • www.zephyrpress.com

Thinking It Over

Which Reach Inside phrase or sentence
do I like best? Why?

_____

_____

_____

_____

_____

What will I do differently next time?

_____

_____

_____

When I use Reach Inside, I am reminded that students . . .

_____

_____

_____

_____

How do my students respond when I Reach Inside?

_____

_____

_____

_____

On a scale of 1 to 10, my students give Reach Inside a _____.

Pick up the Pace

Instead of slowing down to increase comprehension, speed up the tempo of your lesson to increase students' concentration and focus.

Learning has a natural rhythm and flow. It moves and weaves, bobs and dances. Rarely, if ever, is it monotonous or slow. The brain is a complex, highly adaptive organ that has the ability to process information quickly and efficiently (Caine and Caine 1997). Many of us have been told that teaching more slowly increases attention and comprehension, but in fact, we may be teaching too slowly for the brain!

Consider this skiing analogy. Imagine it is a bright, sunny day on the mountain, and fresh, powdery snow covers the slopes. As you head down your first run, you leisurely snowplow back and forth across the snow. You talk with your companions, notice the sun sparkling off the snow in the trees, and smell the crisp, pine-scented air. At this pace you have plenty of time to let your mind wander.

On your second run, your skiing buddy challenges you to race to the lodge. Feeling especially spry you respond with a confident "sure!" and you're off. You tuck your poles and bring your knees together. As your pace increases, your vision narrows and your thoughts focus. You have no time to notice the trees, sky, or pine-scented air. You focus on the snow ahead and anticipate the next turn. With the increased pace, your mind concentrates and your attentiveness heightens.

Picking up the pace of your instruction has a similar effect on the minds of your students. It is possible that the minor disruptions students cause during your lesson might be due to a dragging pace that leaves them with too much time on their brains. Picking up the pace does not mean assigning more work, but rather simply increasing the speed at which you deliver the information. By punctuating the lesson with pauses, checks for understanding, and reminders that they are capable, you can ensure that students stay with you without having to bring the lesson to a halt waiting for every last student to catch up.

Rule of pace: When a majority of the students are ready to move on, do so. The majority will appreciate the quick transition while the others will learn quickly that you and your lessons have a rhythm. Be aware that some students may feel frustrated by the quicker pace. Reassure them that they can and will learn the information, and that you will do whatever you can to assist them.

 When I Pick up the Pace, I increase my students' focus and concentration.

Making It Mine

Consider the pace of your instruction and the flow of activities in your room. Choose a lesson this week and experiment with an upbeat tempo. Let the students know that you plan to Pick up the Pace and that you know they can learn well. Encourage them to ask questions when they need clarification.

Reach for the Stars!

Use the stars below to monitor your progress.

I have this tip down cold!

It is familiar territory.

This tip feels like a new pair of shoes.

If a parent asked you about Pick up the Pace, what would you say? Write your answer here, or if you prefer, draw an icon that represents this HotTip.

Thinking It Over

How did this HotTip increase student
engagement, and how do I know it worked?

_____

_____

_____

_____

_____

What will I do differently next time?

_____

_____

_____

When I use Pick up the Pace, I am reminded that students . . .

_____

_____

_____

The first time I tried Pick up the Pace, my students reacted by . . .

_____

_____

_____

Since then, I have noticed these changes in their reactions.

_____

_____

_____

On a scale of 1 to 10, my students give Pick up the Pace a _____.

Promote Intelligent Student Engagement

Design lessons using strategies compatible with all eight intelligences to maximize students' engagement with the material.

We are enthusiastic about the theory of multiple intelligences (Gardner 1993; Kagan and Kagan 1998) because it provides a language and model for discovering the inner gifts of every child. The greatest contribution to education of this theory is the suggestion that teachers expand their repertoire of techniques, tools, and strategies beyond the typical linguistic and logical modes of presentation. The theory becomes a "meta-model" for organizing and synthesizing new educational innovations ("knowledge lava," if you will). As the plates of change float on a sea of fresh lava, new knowledge emerges. This new knowledge provides a broad range of stimulating curricula to awaken the slumbering brains presently starved for brain-compatible learning.

What follows is a collection of strategies for intelligent engagement. By keeping the multiple intelligences in mind as you design your lessons, you can unleash the myriad potentials within each student. As you experiment with, expand, and explore the following ideas, watch your students come alive!

 I ask myself thought-provoking questions about how to create multiple opportunities for my learners to maximize their engagement with the content.

Making It Mine

VISUAL-SPATIAL

Making It Mine
How can I use visual aids, visualization, color, art, or metaphor?

Making It Theirs
How can they . . .
- use a memory system to learn?
- create a piece of art that demonstrates comprehension?
- vary the color, size, and shape of things?
- color-code a process?
- illustrate, draw, or paint?
- sketch, sculpt, or construct?

Other ideas _____
_____
_____

VERBAL-LINGUISTIC

Making It Mine
How can I use the spoken or written word?

Making It Theirs
How can they . . .
- use storytelling to explain?
- set up a debate?
- lead a class discussion?
- write a letter?
- find synonyms or antonyms?

Other ideas _____
_____
_____
_____
_____

BODILY-KINESTHETIC

Making It Mine
How can I engage the body's capacity for physical learning?

Making It Theirs
How can they . . .
- use hands-on experiences?
- role-play or simulate an event?
- build or construct a model?
- invent a floor or board game?
- create, rehearse, and perform a play?

Other ideas _____
_____
_____

MUSICAL

Making It Mine
How can I use music or environmental sounds, or embed key points in a rhythmic or melodic framework?

Making It Theirs
How can they . . .
- write song lyrics?
- create a musical game?
- use music-production technology?
- make an instrument and use it to demonstrate a concept?
- investigate rhythmical patterns?

Other ideas _____
_____
_____
_____

INTERPERSONAL

Making It Mine
How can I engage students in peer sharing, cooperative learning, and group simulations?

Making It Theirs
How can they . . .
- conduct a class meeting?
- organize or participate in a group?
- use a conflict-management strategy?
- accommodate learning differences?

Other ideas _____
_____
_____
_____

LOGICAL-MATHEMATICAL

Making It Mine
How can I incorporate numbers, calculation, logic, classification, or critical-thinking skills?

Making It Theirs
How can they . . .
- make hypotheses?
- use inductive reasoning?
- use deductive reasoning?
- create a time line?
- interpret data?

Other ideas _____
_____
_____
_____
_____
_____

INTRAPERSONAL

Making It Mine
How can I evoke personal feelings or memories, or give students choices?

Making It Theirs
How can they . . .
- set a goal to accomplish?
- write in a journal?
- explain their intuitive hunches?
- use self-directed learning?
- research and document?

Other ideas _____
_____
_____
_____
_____

NATURALIST

Making It Mine
How can I incorporate the patterns, associations, and themes found in nature?

Making It Theirs
How can they . . .
- forecast?
- simulate the connections between things in nature?
- discover patterns?
- star gaze?
- categorize?

Other ideas _____
_____
_____
_____
_____

Reach for the Stars!

Use the stars below to monitor your progress.

I have this tip
down cold!

It is familiar
territory.

This tip feels like a
new pair of shoes.

If a colleague asked you how you Promote Intelligent Student Engagement, what would you say? Write your answer here, or if you prefer, draw an icon that represents this HotTip.

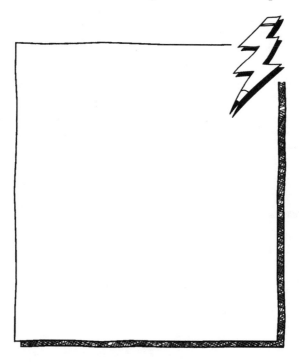

Thinking It Over

Which intelligences do I currently
overutilize in my teaching?

_____

_____

_____

_____

_____

_____

Which intelligences could I tap into more often?

_____

_____

_____

_____

What changes can I make to incorporate these intelligences into
my teaching style?

_____

_____

_____

_____

Which students still are not engaged the way I would like them to
be? What can I do to make learning exciting for them?

_____

_____

_____

_____

Synthesize Learning with KnowBooks

Have students create a book or other collection that represents their knowledge of a topic or unit.

Meaning making is a natural and fundamental function of the brain (Caine and Caine 1994). Drawing on past experience and learning, the brain searches for and creates meaning in every situation. We can capitalize on this innate ability by encouraging students to create a KnowBook.

A KnowBook is a collection of notes, drawings, graphs, pictures, clippings, computer graphics, word-processed text, and the like that represent the knowledge students have accumulated. Think of it as a real-time portfolio of learning, a student-created textbook, a learning scrapbook, and a memento of learning. The KnowBook can be a three-ring binder, an 8 1/2" x 11" sketchbook from the art supply store, or a picture album. It contains a title page (for example, "Lynn's KnowBook") and a page for the table of contents (written when the KnowBook is completed). It is best if students do most of the writing and drawing themselves rather than simply cutting and pasting from other sources.

What might pages in the KnowBook contain?

> ➤ Handwritten notes (color-coded to assist memory) from a lecture, or information gleaned from a textbook, encyclopedias, or the Internet

- Diagrams illustrating processes such as the water cycle, how to solve a particular math problem, or the forms of plate tectonics, each labeled with pertinent information
- Summaries or reflections about a topic
- Cartoons explaining what the student learned
- Stories narrating "A Day in the Life of . . ." (a Beetle, a Variable, an Amoeba)
- Vocabulary picture-words in which the word is written to resemble a drawing that conveys its meaning

 Using KnowBooks allows my students to make meaning for themselves and capture their learning.

Making It Mine

Your next unit or lesson might be the perfect opportunity for students to create their own KnowBooks. Ask yourself, "What would be the best form for this collection of knowledge?" Then ask, "In what ways could students best represent this knowledge? Should they follow a prescribed format or be free to create their own, within certain guidelines? How often will they add to their KnowBooks?"

Let your students' creative juices loose! As you can imagine, the possibilities are endless. If you ever run out of ideas, simply ask the students to capture what they know about the topic in their own way! Be prepared for incredible creativity!

Reach for the Stars!

Use the stars below to monitor your progress.

I have this tip down cold!

It is familiar territory.

This tip feels like a new pair of shoes.

If a classroom visitor asked you about the students' KnowBooks, what would you say? Write your answer here, or if you prefer, draw an icon that represents this HotTip.

HotTips for Teachers ©2002 Zephyr Press, Chicago, IL • (800) 232-2187 • www.zephyrpress.com

Thinking It Over

What have I found to be the best use of
KnowBooks?

_____

_____

_____

_____

What are my plans for Synthesizing Learning with KnowBooks
in future lessons?

_____

_____

_____

_____

When I Synthesize Learning with KnowBooks, I am reminded that
students . . .

_____

_____

_____

_____

What do my students have to say about Synthesize Learning with
KnowBooks?

_____

_____

_____

_____

On a scale of 1 to 10, my students give Synthesize Learning with
KnowBooks a _____.

Leave Open Loops

Give students a tidbit of forthcoming information so they anticipate and listen for the rest (the close of the loop).

Look at the picture on this page. What is it? If you are like most people, you will immediately respond, "a circle," but on closer inspection, notice that it is actually an open or incomplete circle. Why was your first reaction a circle? Because the human brain seeks closure, completeness, and wholeness. In its attempt to create meaning, the brain closed the gap and identified the shape as a circle.

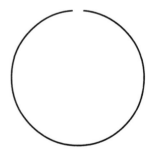

Here is an interesting question: What effect might the concept of "open loops" (a phrase coined by our friend and fellow facilitator Rich Allen) have on students' attention and interest? How can we capitalize on the brain's insatiable desire to seek meaning in order to gain closure? Here is how: Novelty and intrigue are two of the brain's favorite snacks. It eats them up like the Cookie Monster devours cookies. We can increase our students' appetites by momentarily withholding bits of information. Since the brain can parallel-process, students stay focused on what you are teaching while in the background they anticipate the next morsel of information (Caine and Caine 1994, 88).

Here are a few statements that create an open loop:

- ➤ "The step just before the last one is 'invert.'" (math)
- ➤ "They were in for the ultimate loss, but we'll get to that in just a moment. First, Germany was in big trouble." (history)
- ➤ "Wow! What an idea, Brooke! Hold on to that thought. We'll explain why those pennies float in just one minute." (science)
- ➤ "We'll be right back with more on those dangling participles." (English)
- ➤ "Coming soon to a class near you!" (general)

Just be sure to remember to close the open loop in a timely manner. In doing so, you build rapport by demonstrating your reliability.

 By Leaving Open Loops, I build anticipation and interest for what's coming next.

Making It Mine

Where in your next lesson could you use an open loop? In the introduction? During the middle of instruction? In the closing as a teaser for the next lesson? Or perhaps you already are Leaving Open Loops.

Take a moment right now and create three open loops you could use tomorrow.

1. _____
   _____ .

2. _____
   _____ .

3. _____
   _____ .

Reach for the Stars!

Use the stars below to monitor your progress.

I have this tip down cold!

It is familiar territory.

This tip feels like a new pair of shoes.

If a new teacher asked you about Leave Open Loops, what would you say? Write your answer here, or if you prefer, draw an icon that represents this HotTip.

HotTips for Teachers ©2002 Zephyr Press, Chicago, IL • (800) 232-2187 • www.zephyrpress.com

Thinking It Over

What positive changes did I notice
when I tried Leave Open Loops?

_____

_____

_____

_____

_____

_____

What will I do differently next time?

_____

_____

_____

_____

When I Leave Open Loops, I am reminded that students . . .

_____

_____

_____

_____

What difference have I noticed in my students since I have been
consciously Leaving Open Loops?

_____

_____

_____

_____

On a scale of 1 to 10, my students give Leave Open Loops a _____.

Dramatize Your Point

Do something a little unusual to add novelty to key points so students remember them.

Crazy. Funny. Wacky. Weird. Out-of-the-ordinary. What do these words and phrases have in common? The brain remembers them! Novelty is fuel for the brain (Jensen 1995). By taking the ordinary and making it extraordinary, the mundane and making it insane (or a little quirky at least), we heighten students' interest and retention.

In the movie *Dead Poets Society*, Robin Williams masterfully employed the strategy of Dramatize Your Point. One of the most memorable scenes places us in the foyer outside his classroom. After a few leading questions based on a text read by a student, he invites the class to a trophy case lined with old photos. He says to the class, "If you really listen closely . . . That's right, lean in." A few of the students look a bit confused but lean in anyway. Everyone is expectant, silent. "Listen. Do you hear it?" From behind them, he whispers in a slow, low tone, "Car–pe . . . car–pe . . . carpe diem. Seize the day, boys. Make your lives extraordinary."

He could have said "carpe diem" in a normal tone of voice and written it on an overhead. He could have stood behind a lectern and delivered an elegant speech, expounding on the historical and linguistic characteristics of the phrase and its philosophical ramifications. But no! He huddles the students up, draws them in close, and at the peak of interest, delivers the phrase with finesse.

Did he overdo it? Did he give in to the need to entertain? Perhaps. But more important, he employed elements that the brain craves and crafted them to make the content stick in his students' minds.

Here are a few ways you can dramatize your point:

- Whisper it.
- Shout it!
- Pause just before you say it.
- Precede it with a drum roll.
- Precede it with a fanfare.
- Reveal it slowly on the overhead.
- Clang a bell.
- Write it on the board in tiny letters.
- Write it on the board in huge letters.
- Write it in the air.
- Sing it (see also Campbell 1992).
- Rap it.
- Pantomime it.

 I increase my students' ability to remember the information when I Dramatize My Point.

Making It Mine

What is the most important word, phrase, or idea in your next lesson? What would be the best way to make it novel or intriguing? Experiment with a variety of strategies until you find the best one for that point in that particular lesson. Carry out your idea with panache.

Point: _____

_____

_____

How to dramatize: _____

_____

_____

Reach for the Stars! ✩ ✦ ✦ ✦ ✦

Use the stars below to monitor your progress.

I have this tip down cold!

It is familiar territory.

This tip feels like a new pair of shoes.

If a colleague asked you about Dramatize Your Point, what would you say? Write your answer here, or if you prefer, draw an icon that represents this HotTip.

Thinking It Over

What has been my favorite dramatic
strategy? Why?

_____

_____

_____

_____

_____

Which new strategy would stretch me beyond my comfort zone?
(Choose a time when it will debut and go for it!)

_____

_____

_____

_____

When I use Dramatize Your Point, I am reminded that students . . .

_____

_____

_____

_____

Have my students noticed me using Dramatize Your Point? How
do I know?

_____

_____

_____

_____

On a scale of 1 to 10, my students give Dramatize Your Point a

_____.

Put the Content in Motion

Create specific movements to represent
key points, to draw on students' muscle
memory.

What do professional athletes, actors, speakers, musicians, and your students have in common? They use their bodies to remember. They capitalize on the power of muscle memory by accessing the kinesthetic modality.

A content motion is a gesture or movement related to a key concept in the lesson or unit. By associating specific content with a motion, we invite students to participate in the lesson and strengthen their ability to remember the information. Hand signals, arm movements, body postures, and even dances can grab students' attention and cement the learning into their muscle memory. (Besides, boredom arises in part from lack of movement. Students who are moving are less likely to be bored!)

Imagine that your students are learning long division. The words *divide, multiply, subtract,* and *bring down* summarize the four steps. Use your fingers and hands to represent the four operations. As you teach the four steps, encourage students to do each hand motion as they say the operation. You could even set the four motions to music and do the "Long Division Hand Jive"!

Content motions are applicable to all content areas. For example:

Science: phases of cell division, Newton's three laws, the water cycle

Geography: map projections, cardinal points, land formations

History: the three branches of U.S. government, types of governments, imperialism, industrialism

Math: multiplying positive and negative numbers, geometric shapes, "invert and multiply," "PEMDAS" (the order of operations in algebra)

English: prepositions, three main parts of an essay, plot structure

Use your fingers, hands, and body to represent each key idea visually and kinesthetically, keeping in mind the following two principles:

1. Be selective. Use content motions for the significant concepts or for areas where students are often confused.
2. Make each motion distinctive in terms of speed or position, and add a sound or word to each.

 Attaching key concepts to body motions helps my students participate and remember.

Making It Mine

Capture the power of the mind-body connection by creating content motions for your subject. Consider a lesson you will be teaching soon. What are the key points? How could using hand, arm, or body motions represent each of those?

Key Point	**Content Motion**
_____	_____
_____	_____
_____	_____
_____	_____

Do the motions until they become second nature for you. Your ease and confidence with each content motion will influence your students' willingness to participate.

Reach for the Stars!

Use the stars below to monitor your progress.

I have this tip
down cold!

It is familiar
territory.

This tip feels like a
new pair of shoes.

If an administrator asked you about Put the Content in Motion,
what would you say? Write your answer here, or if you prefer,
draw an icon that represents this HotTip.

Thinking It Over

What positive changes did I notice
when I Put the Content in Motion?

_____

_____

_____

_____

_____

_____

What will I do differently next time?

_____

_____

_____

_____

When I Put the Content in Motion, I am reminded that students . . .

_____

_____

_____

_____

What do my students say about Put the Content in Motion?

_____

_____

_____

_____

On a scale of 1 to 10, my students give Put the Content in Motion
a _____.

Engage Your Heart

Cultivate emotional intelligence in yourself and your students through your everyday actions.

It may be wise, even essential for the success of the planet, to cultivate an intelligence deep within us, an intelligence that some speculate actually orchestrates the other intelligences (Goleman 1997, 2000). This intelligence is that of the heart. It orients us toward the common good of humankind, permeating our actions, governing our conscience, and connecting us to one another.

One of the most intelligent things we can do as continuous learners is to cultivate this superordinate heart intelligence—first exploring it within ourselves, and then assisting our learners to do the same. We must connect to their hearts. We must model this intelligence for them. We must be heart-minded.

Research into emotional intelligence over the past five years has documented the importance of the heart in teaching and learning. Emotional intelligence theory has radically influenced our intentions as we deliver information and the ways in which we deliver that information (Goleman 2000). We have rediscovered that the connection to our learners is through their hearts. By approaching the heart first, we can enter and enrich our learners' minds.

Here are a few pathways into the life and heart of a child:

The power of presence. Be with your students. Invest your time, because what they really want most is your presence.

Your artful connection of the cognitive to the kinesthetic. Provoke their thinking. Give caring touch in age-appropriate ways. Listen attentively and respond with positive affect. Touch their hearts.

The deposition of values and lifelong learning. Influence their future every day of your life by being the best role model you can.

Display these heart characteristics as often and freely as you can: care, compassion, forgiveness, understanding, patience, kindness, humor, and appreciation.

 By connecting with my students' hearts I build rapport, engage emotions, and increase learning.

Making It Mine

Here are three heart objectives to consider every day:

1. What can I do every day so that my students experience and discover the joy of learning?

_____

_____

_____

2. What can I do today to inspire my students' dreams?

_____

_____

_____

3. What can I offer students today that will ignite their passion and turn their dreams to action?

_____

_____

_____

Reach for the Stars!

Use the stars below to monitor your progress.

I have this tip
down cold!

It is familiar
territory.

This tip feels like a
new pair of shoes.

If a parent asked you about Engage Your Heart, what would you say? Write your answer here, or if you prefer, draw an icon that represents this HotTip.

HotTips for Teachers ©2002 Zephyr Press, Chicago, IL • (800) 232-2187 • www.zephyrpress.com

Thinking It Over

What aspects of this HotTip were
successful, and how could I tell?

_____

_____

_____

_____

_____

_____

What will I do differently next time?

_____

_____

_____

_____

When I Engage My Heart, I am reminded that students . . .

_____

_____

_____

_____

What differences have I noticed in my students since I've been
consciously using Engage Your Heart?

_____

_____

_____

_____

On a scale of 1 to 10, my students give Engage Your Heart a _____.

Regain Focus
with Diffusers

Break up your lesson with short activities
that use a different modality, intelligence,
or skill, to let students' brains "shift gear."

Now you have them. Now you don't. Students' attention spans are much like that. One moment we seem to have them in the palms of our hands. The next, we're wondering who tampered with their heads. How can we maximize students' attentiveness without burning them out? The concept of diffusers can help.

The brain operates in alternating cycles of activity and rest, fluctuating in a natural rhythm (Jensen 1994). Prolonged periods of focus that are not aligned with the brain's organic need for variety are actually detrimental to comprehension and retention. Use this formula to determine how long your students can remain on task:

Age of Brain = Minutes of Focus ± 2

Take the average age of your students. That number plus or minus two is the appropriate number of minutes you can expect them to focus. Let's say you teach eighth grade. The average age of an eighth grader is 13. You can expect these students to stay engaged for about 11 to 15 minutes. Then their brains need a diffuser to regain focus; namely, a one- to three-minute activity related to the topic that utilizes a different skill, intelligence, or modality.

Here are a few possible diffusers:

- ➤ Discuss today's topic with your neighbor.
- ➤ Highlight your notes.
- ➤ Summarize the last point in one word.
- ➤ Draw a symbol for each main point.
- ➤ Stand and review your notes with a partner.
- ➤ Pretend you are a _____ (for example, water molecule during condensation, early European American settler in Kansas).
- ➤ Take the opposite viewpoint and defend it.

 I can maximize my students' ability to focus by employing diffusers.

Making It Mine

In each "focus" box below, write the average number of minutes your students can be expected to stay focused. In each "diffuser" section, write one activity you could use in an upcoming lesson (you may want to write sideways). Remember: Variety is the spice of life!

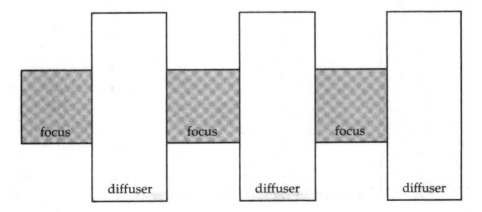

focus   focus   focus

diffuser   diffuser   diffuser

Reach for the Stars!

Use the stars below to monitor your progress.

**I have this tip
down cold!**

**It is familiar
territory.**

**This tip feels like a
new pair of shoes.**

If a master teacher asked how you Regain Focus with Diffusers, what would you say? Write your answer here, or if you prefer, draw an icon that represents this HotTip.

Thinking It Over

What diffusers have worked the best for my
students and me? How do I know they worked?

_____

_____

_____

_____

_____

_____

What will I do differently next time?

_____

_____

_____

_____

When I Regain Focus with Diffusers, I am reminded that students . . .

_____

_____

_____

_____

What changes in my students have I noticed since using Regain
Focus with Diffusers?

_____

_____

_____

_____

On a scale of 1 to 10, my students give Regain Focus with Diffusers
a _____.

Interject State Changers

Break up the lesson with brief movements or actions to change students' psychological states.

The brain is amazing! It constantly seeks out new challenges, boldly going where no brain has gone before! It craves stimulation and novelty, discovering new ways to use its creative abilities.

So what happens when the brain perceives the current lesson to be less than challenging? You got it! The brain seeks out stimulation. This shows up in a variety of ways—talking with a neighbor, writing notes, teasing the neighboring student, and making humorous comments. What would class be like if you could keep students' brains focused and attentive? Could you teach better with increased results? Without a doubt!

Jensen (1995) suggests that all learning is state dependent. By facilitating students' state, otherwise known as their psycho-physiological condition, we can maintain their interest. Think of state as a snapshot of a mood. There are many different kinds of states: confused, creative, alert, interested, intrigued, frustrated, bored, fascinated, and cooperative. States are neither good nor bad in and of themselves, but some states are more useful than others for learning.

Since the body and mind are connected, moving the body can recapture the mind, a strategy we call "state changers." Here are a few of our favorite ways to regain or maintain resourceful learning states.

Have your students

> ➤ take a big deep breath and exhale slowly.
> ➤ switch seats to gain a fresh perspective.
> ➤ stand and take a bow as you applaud.
> ➤ stand up and stretch.
> ➤ sit up tall and lean forward.
> ➤ clap three times.
> ➤ shout the answer.
> ➤ whisper the answer.
> ➤ stand up for the next part of the lesson.
> ➤ use a content motion (see page 76).

 When I facilitate students' psychological state, I enhance their attention.

Making It Mine

Take a stack of ten 3" x 5" cards and write one state changer on each card. Keep the cards close at hand (on your desk, or on the chalk or pen tray). When you notice students' attention waning, pull out a card and change their state.

Match the state change with your desired outcome. If the tone at that point in the lesson is reflective, use a deep breath. If the tone is more lively, have them stand up. Your goal is to facilitate students' psychological state so that they maintain the optimal frame of mind.

Reach for the Stars!

Use the stars below to monitor your progress.

I have this tip
down cold!

It is familiar
territory.

This tip feels like a
new pair of shoes.

If a school board member asked you about Interject State Changers, what would you say? Write your answer here, or if you prefer, draw an icon that represents this HotTip.

Thinking It Over

What state changers work best for my
students and me? How do I know they work?

_____

_____

_____

_____

_____

_____

Invent three new state changers. (If you need help, ask a student!)

1. _____

2. _____

3. _____

When I Interject State Changers, I am reminded that students . . .

_____

_____

_____

_____

What do my students say about Interject State Changers?

_____

_____

_____

_____

On a scale of 1 to 10, my students give Interject State Changers a

_____.

Make Call Backs

Punctuate key points by interjecting questions that have students repeat the information in unison.

This strategy capitalizes on the brain's desire to answer questions and students' desire to participate. Call backs can be used at any time throughout the lesson to highlight or punctuate key points, important vocabulary, or vital steps in directions. Here are examples:

Teacher: There are three main parts to an essay: the introduction, the body, and the conclusion. How many parts are there?

Students: Three.

Teacher: The introduction includes at least two things: a hook and the thesis statement, which is your opinion about the topic. In the introduction, you grab the readers' attention and tell them your opinion of the topic. So, you need two things: a hook and a thesis. What two things do you need in the introduction?

Students: A hook and a thesis.

Here is another example when giving directions:

Teacher: We'll do two things before we dismiss for lunch. When I say, "spaghetti" . . . When I say what?

Students: Spaghetti.

Teacher: Put away your materials and be ready to name today's theme. What two things will you do?

Students: Put away our materials and say today's theme.

Teacher: Perfect. Spaghetti!

This is a simple yet powerful way to keep students' minds engaged on the lesson while boosting recognition and recall of important concepts. A word of caution: Use this HotTip sparingly! Make Call Backs only for your most salient points.

 By Making Call Backs, I focus students' attention on key words and concepts.

Making It Mine

What are the most important words or concepts you want students to remember in your next lesson? Go ahead and jot them down. Now imagine yourself teaching the lesson and Making Call Backs to emphasis the key points.

_____

_____

_____

_____

_____

_____

_____

_____

Reach for the Stars!

Use the stars below to monitor your progress.

**I have this tip
down cold!**

**It is familiar
territory.**

**This tip feels like a
new pair of shoes.**

If a colleague asked you about Make Call Backs, what would you say? Write your answer here, or if you prefer, draw an icon that represents this HotTip.

Thinking It Over

Which of my call backs worked best, and
how do I know?

_____

_____

_____

_____

_____

_____

What will I do differently next time?

_____

_____

_____

_____

When I Make Call Backs, I am reminded that students . . .

_____

_____

_____

_____

What changes have I noticed in my students since I began Making
Call Backs?

_____

_____

_____

_____

On a scale of 1 to 10, my students give Make Call Backs a _____.

Elicit Thinking

Use a five-step process for asking questions: set the context, prompt, ask the question, pause, and elicit several answers.

The brain needs time to think. It needs time to make meaning of new information or experiences. To prove this point, let's do a simple experiment. Read as quickly as you can: Imagine you are looking at a blank sheet of notebook paper. What color is it? What do cows drink?

Did you say to yourself, "Milk"? But cows drink water! Even with those two simple questions, your brain needed a bit more time to think clearly, to generate the appropriate associations, and to retrieve the answer.

Elicit Thinking is a strategy that allows students to process information before you call on them for an answer. It works like this:

1. **Set the context:** "We've been discussing the steps in the scientific method."

2. **Prompt:** "Think for a moment about those steps and their order."

3. **Ask the question:** "What are the steps in the scientific method?"

4. **Pause:** Wait for three to five seconds to give everyone an opportunity to formulate the answer.

5. **Elicit thinking:** Call on a variety of students, even if the first one gives the right answer. Acknowledge each student

with a simple, "Thank you." After three to five students have answered, respond with, "If you said or were thinking _____, you were right!" Alternatively, you could take a vote to determine agreement or even have students defend the answer they think is correct. By calling on many students, you sample the general depth of understanding in the class and send a message that everyone needs to be thinking.

In our need to cover content quickly, we often ask rapid-fire questions and expect students to respond in like fashion. A simple reminder: *We* know the content already; *they* are just learning it! We can honor the learning process by using Elicit Thinking as our guide.

Now you might be thinking, "What do I do about those students who always raise their hands or who blurt out the answer?" Play the "be ready" game. Here's how it works: Just before you ask the question say, "Be ready when I call on you to give the answer." The message is simple but powerful. In essence, you are saying, "If you showed up today . . . tag, you're it! No one sits on the sidelines. Everyone is eligible to play." Using the "be ready" game ensures that every student must be prepared to answer the question.

"But, wait," you say, "what do I do when I call on a student who answers, 'I don't know'?" Even though you have prompted students' thinking, someone might say, "I don't know." Rather than play mind reader by attempting to discern the truthfulness of this statement, simply supply the student with an alternative. Instead of "I don't know," the student must respond with one of these four answers:

1. "Would you please repeat the question?"
2. "I would like to review my notes."
3. "I need more time to think."
4. "I'd like to confer with a classmate."

The key is in facilitating this moment. Regardless of the student's response you say, "I'll be right back." Then call on another student and return to Mr. or Ms. I-Don't-Know. This strategy tells students that their thinking is worth your time and attention, and that thinking is an important part of participating.

 I enhance my students' thinking and their participation by giving them time to think.

Making It Mine

How can you graft this HotTip onto your natural teaching style? First, review the steps of Elicit Thinking. Now envision yourself in your classroom, at the moment when you will be asking questions. Remind students what they have been learning. Then prompt their  thinking before you ask the question. Remind them to be ready when you call on them. Now ask the question, refraining from calling on a particular student. Feel yourself waiting for about three to five seconds as students gather their thoughts. Go around the room, eliciting answers from a number of students. Acknowledge their responses but do not correct them, then confirm the right answer. You'll find students' ability to think clearly will increase and so will class participation.

Reach for the Stars!

Use the stars below to monitor your progress.

I have this tip down cold!

It is familiar territory.

This tip feels like a new pair of shoes.

HotTips for Teachers ©2002 Zephyr Press, Chicago, IL • (800) 232-2187 • www.zephyrpress.com

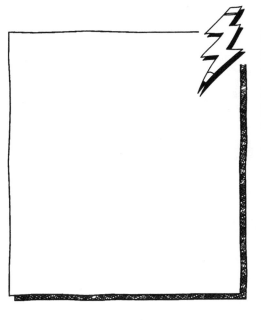

If a student teacher asked you about Elicit Thinking, what would you say? Write your answer here, or if you prefer, draw an icon that represents this HotTip.

Thinking It Over

What aspects of Elicit Thinking did I implement successfully?

_____

_____

_____

What will I do differently next time?

_____

_____

_____

How has the quality of my students' answers changed since I started Eliciting Thinking?

_____

_____

_____

Ask for Classwide Signaling

 Have the whole class give feedback about their comprehension with hand signals or other nonverbal responses.

Wouldn't it be great if we had the ability to read our students' minds—if we could actually get inside their heads to know how they are processing our teaching? With that telepathic ability, we would know with certainty how each individual student was doing. Well, until that day arrives, we must settle for a less-refined "body-pathic" technology. Students can signal their answers, intentions, and thinking by using their fingers, a hand, an arm, or a card.

How does this HotTip work? Imagine you are halfway through the lesson and wish to check the students' understanding. You would say, "Please show thumbs up if you completely understand, thumbs down if you're lost, and thumbs to the side if you need more explanation or practice." With a quick glance, you get immediate feedback while requesting participation from everyone.

Sign language is useful as well. Imagine you're in class conducting a discussion, and students are eagerly participating. Some students want to ask *questions,* others have *comments,* and others want to give the *answer.* Request that students show the sign-language letter for the type of contribution they want to make (Q for *question,* C for *comment,* or A for *answer*).

Here are other ways of signaling:

- ➤ Show the mathematical operation used to solve the problem with finger/hand combinations.
- ➤ Represent the number of the question you missed using your fingers.
- ➤ Indicate your understanding by raising your hand to a high, middle, or low level.
- ➤ Everyone write the answer on your mini-slate or white board.
- ➤ Represent a particular molecular, geometric, or mathematical property with numbered tiles.
- ➤ Spell words with lettered tiles.

Talk to your students about the importance of honest signaling. Explain that the reason you are asking for a signal is so you can get the feedback you need to do a better job of teaching.

I raise the level of accountability each time I ask students to give me a signal.

Making It Mine

Which of the preceding strategies would you feel comfortable doing? When in your next lesson would be the most appropriate time to insert that signaling technique?

Strategy: _____

_____

_____

Time to use: _____

_____

_____

Reach for the Stars!

Use the stars below to monitor your progress.

I have this tip
down cold!

It is familiar
territory.

This tip feels like a
new pair of shoes.

If a student asked why you Ask for Classwide Signaling, what would you say? Write your answer here, or if you prefer, draw an icon that represents this HotTip.

HotTips for Teachers ©2002 Zephyr Press, Chicago, IL • (800) 232-2187 • www.zephyrpress.com

Thinking It Over

What classwide signaling technique (or techniques) works best to get the feedback I need about my students' levels of under- standing?

_____

_____

_____

_____

_____

What new signals could I try next time?

_____

_____

_____

_____

When I Ask for Classwide Signaling, I am reminded that students . . .

_____

_____

_____

_____

What do my students say about Ask for Classwide Signaling?

_____

_____

_____

_____

On a scale of 1 to 10, my students give Ask for Classwide Signaling a _____.

Box Their Understanding

Have students use visual representations, such as icons on cards, to give you feedback about their level of understanding.

Sometimes the physical cues students give us during the lesson can be misleading. A seemingly expressionless face could be an indication of complete understanding, and a smile could be the mask of confusion. To gain a more accurate indication of each student's understanding, use boxes to represent comprehension. Request that each student choose the one box that best represents his or her current level of understanding. (See below.) In the early grades, students might hold up a prepared index card with the appropriate box. Students in upper grades could show their level of understanding on their fingers (1 = lost, 2 = hazy, and so on).

LOST
Not even sure
what question
to ask.

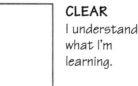

HAZY
I have a
question.

CLEAR
I understand
what I'm
learning.

OWN IT!
I could teach
this to
someone else.

Sometimes we do not catch the "lost" students until well into the lesson. By Boxing Their Understanding, students can maintain a sense of anonymity and not embarrass themselves by admitting out loud that they are lost. At the same time, you can instantly spot those who feel they can teach others (ownership) and pair them with those who have yet to gain mastery.

 I can gain instant feedback regarding students' comprehension when I ask them to  Box Their Understanding.

Making It Mine

Draw four boxes on a large piece of construction paper. Label them "1. Lost," "2. Hazy," "3. Clear," and "4. Own it!" Place the paper at the front of the room or near the front on a side wall.

For little ones, you could draw an icon for each level of understanding on an index card (in black and white). Then place the four cards on a copy machine that takes card stock. Copy one set for each student and cut apart to make a personal set of cards.

Explain to class members that they can contribute to how well you teach by providing feedback during the lesson. Let them know that throughout the day's lessons, you will ask them to indicate their level of understanding. You will use this information to adjust the flow and depth of the lesson so that everyone can learn as quickly as possible.

Reach for the Stars! ★ ★ ★ ✦ ★

Use the stars below to monitor your progress.

**I have this tip
down cold!**

**It is familiar
territory.**

**This tip feels like a
new pair of shoes.**

If your superintendent asked you about Box Their Understanding, what would you say? Write your answer here, or if you prefer, draw an icon that represents this HotTip.

Thinking It Over

What useful feedback did I get from using Box
Their Understanding?

_____

_____

_____

_____

_____

_____

What will I do differently next time?

_____

_____

_____

_____

When I Box Their Understanding, I am reminded that students . . .

_____

_____

_____

_____

What do my students say about Box Their Understanding?

_____

_____

_____

_____

On a scale of 1 to 10, my students give Box Their Understanding a

_____.

Find Synection, the Ultimate in Engagement

Plan for moments of complete engagement.

We describe "synection" (from *synergy* + *connection*) as the moment when the students are engaged synergistically with the activity of the moment. This is the moment when the light bulbs go on in students' heads. Such a moment cannot be measured on a standardized test or quantified in a report, but without it, each day in class becomes just another day. It is synection that keeps us engaged in learning, engaged in life.

 Today I will plan for moments of synection.

Making It Mine

On the following pages are cognitive and meta-cognitive questions that support you in thinking of ways to facilitate engagement with your learners. Consider each question carefully before you begin your teaching day or individual lesson. Use them as guides for creating synergy and connection with your students.

- What kind of music is playing in the background? Baroque, nature sounds, soft rock?
- How can I thank and acknowledge my students?
- What will my first three sentences be?
- How will I grab students' attention and jump-start them into the lesson?
- What reason will I give them for being here? What's in it for them? How is what I am teaching important?

- Am I natural and relaxed? What messages might my body be revealing?
- How is my state? Am I tired, enthusiastic, or somewhere in between?
- Can I connect with each of my students using empathetic eye contact?
- What will I do to breathe "fresh air" into my delivery? Could I use quotations, cartoons, stories, humor, or demonstrations?
- How can I keep students' attention piqued?
- How will I punctuate my content?

- What will be the level of students' involvement today?
- When will I talk less and let them do more?
- Have I incorporated a role for several different intelligences within the structure of the lesson or day? What opportunities are built into the lesson or day for students to read, talk, write, draw, sketch, visualize, work in a group, sing, dance, use their hands, conceptualize, and quantify?

> ➤ In what ways have I provided my students with sufficient time for group debriefing and personal reflection?
> ➤ How will I make the closing of my day or lesson memorable?
> ➤ How can I review the day for students in three short sentences?

> ➤ How many smiles and how much laughter will fill the air?
> ➤ In what ways can I be my natural self in front of my class?
> ➤ How can I reveal the real me to them?
> ➤ How can I show them that I care for them?
> ➤ What can I do to display my sense of humor and tap into theirs?
> ➤ How will I show my love for learning?

Reach for the Stars!

Use the stars below to monitor your progress.

I have this tip down cold!

It is familiar territory.

This tip feels like a new pair of shoes.

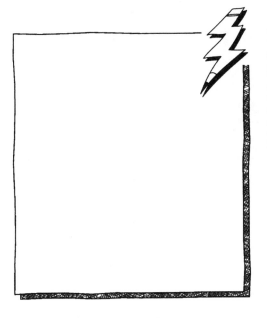

If your student teacher asked you about Find Synection, what would you say? Write your answer here, or if you prefer, draw an icon that represents this HotTip.

Thinking It Over

Where were the high points in the lesson or day, and what made them successful?

_____

_____

_____

Where were the low points in the class or day, the times when the students needed a spark?

_____

_____

_____

What will I do differently to turn boredom into learning epiphany?

_____

_____

_____

Listen-Write

Students listen with pencils down while you present a chunk of information. Then they write the key points and verify them with a partner.

What would class be like if students listened more attentively? What effect would that have on their comprehension? On their mastery of your content? Do we even need to ask?

Listen-Write is an effective way to improve students' listening comprehension and develop their ability to analyze. Have students listen first, encouraging them to listen intently. Then they must determine what is most important and write it down. Specifically, Listen-Write works like this:

1. Tell your students that you will be teaching in a different way today, to help them become better listeners. Elicit reasons why being a good listener is important.

2. Explain that you will be giving information in small chunks, much like eating a bag of potato chips one chip at a time. While you are talking, they are to be listening carefully for the most important word, phrase, or idea. After a few minutes, you'll stop to give them an opportunity to write down what they heard.

3. After students have written down what they heard, have them share with a partner what they wrote. They are to check for accuracy, each making corrections on his or her own paper if necessary.

4. Next, have students put their pens or pencils down and listen while you continue with the next chunk. After a few minutes, they write what they think was the most important information.

You may want to appoint a timer to help you stay on track with each chunk. Remember: Keep the pace moving.

Note: When students are first learning Listen-Write, it is helpful to tell them what you expected them to write on their paper. Providing the answer validates those who caught the key points and gives immediate feedback to the others.

 I improve my students' ability to listen carefully when I use Listen-Write.

Making It Mine

For what portion of your content might Listen-Write work best? What modifications would you make to better meet the needs of your students?

Best uses: _____

_____

_____

_____

Modifications: _____

_____

_____

_____

Reach for the Stars!

Use the stars below to monitor your progress.

I have this tip down cold!

It is familiar territory.

This tip feels like a new pair of shoes.

If a colleague asked you about Listen-Write, what would you say? Write your answer here, or if you prefer, draw an icon that represents this HotTip.

Thinking It Over

What worked well, and how do I know it
worked?

_____

_____

_____

_____

_____

_____

What will I do differently next time?

_____

_____

_____

_____

When I use Listen-Write, I am reminded that students . . .

_____

_____

_____

_____

What improvements have my students demonstrated since they
have been using Listen-Write?

_____

_____

_____

_____

On a scale of 1 to 10, my students give Listen-Write a _____.

Draw on Guided Peer Teaching

 Divide students into pairs, then teach a chunk of information to one partner. The partner assumes the role of teacher in presenting the information to the second student.

Do you want to facilitate students' ability to grasp, articulate, and retain new information? Eric Jensen (1994), noted translator of brain research into educational practice, suggests that participants who talk about their learning learn it better. In guided peer teaching, participants articulate what they know to a peer. In doing so, they rehearse the new information and gain confidence in their ability to talk about the subject matter.

Guided peer teaching capitalizes on two components necessary to increase comprehension and retention. The first is rehearsal. By sharing new information with someone else, the learners craft personal meaning while articulating what they now know. The second is role-play. Assuming the personae of individuals known for their intelligence and ability calls upon the brain to perform at a higher, more integrated level. Our experience shows that when learners "act as if," they become more intelligent, wiser, more distinguished, and more important.

Here is the guided peer teaching process:

1. To begin, each student chooses a partner. The partners agree to take on the roles of famous people, such as noted scientists, researchers, explorers, mathematicians, artists, musicians, or writers. For ease of explanation, let's say Einstein and Madame Curie.

2. Explain to everyone that you'll teach small chunks of information to one person (Einstein) of the pair. While you are teaching the group of Einsteins, the partners (the Mesdames Curie) remain at their desks. When each chunk is complete, it is Einstein's responsibility to share what he now knows with his partner (Curie), who in turn creates her own notes.

3. What does the waiting student (Madame Curie) do while Einstein is learning from you? She remains seated, is silent, and does her very best not to listen to the sound of your voice! Since you will be teaching for only about two to four minutes, she will hardly know she was not paying attention! She could also be allowed free reading time, challenged to solve a logic puzzle in her head, or given a quick activity break to "shift gears." (See Regain Focus with Diffusers on page 84.)

4. When the first round is complete, it is Madame Curie's turn to receive the next chunk of information and explain it to Einstein.

5. You might be concerned that the information may not be shared correctly as it passes from you through another student. Between rounds, either check for understanding or conduct a quick review of the most salient points.

As variations of this HotTip, you could pair up students with different intelligence strengths to teach each other different subjects—for example, a student who is strong in the naturalist intelligence could be the peer teacher for biology, and her partner, strong in the logical-mathematical intelligence, could teach algebra. Peer teaching can also provide a novel way for students to review for a test.

I increase students' access to and retention of information each time I use Guided Peer Teaching.

Making It Mine

Consider an upcoming lesson where Draw on Guided Peer Teaching might be appropriate. Examples might be a lesson that has steps—such as solving a math problem—or stages—such as the process of cell division. As you look over the content, notice where you could chunk the information. Accentuate the information with visuals (see page 26) and possible hand/body motions (see page 76) that would aid in retention.

Now choose which famous scientists, mathematicians, artists, philosophers, explorers, or whomever your students will personify as they learn and rehearse the new information. Finally, remind yourself to review between each transition to ensure everyone captures the information correctly.

Reach for the Stars!

Use the stars below to monitor your progress.

I have this tip down cold!

It is familiar territory.

This tip feels like a new pair of shoes.

HotTips for Teachers ©2002 Zephyr Press, Chicago, IL • (800) 232-2187 • www.zephyrpress.com

If a master teacher asked how you Draw on Guided Peer Teaching, what would you say? Write your answer here, or if you prefer, draw an icon that represents this HotTip.

Thinking It Over

Did guided peer teaching work well? How do I know?

_____

_____

_____

Did participants lose interest or focus at any point? What could I do to increase their interest and focus?

_____

_____

_____

What changes in my students have I noticed since Drawing on Guided Peer Teaching?

_____

_____

_____

On a scale of 1 to 10, my students give Draw on Guided Peer Teaching a _____.

Bring Me Your Brains

Have students work in teams to teach each other segments of a lesson.

This large-group guided tutoring activity develops thinking skills, fosters teamwork, and develops interpersonal communication skills. (It's a natural fit for your students who are strong in interpersonal intelligence.) Use the following format to guide you.

1. Divide the content into between two and four sections and divide the class into teams of four or five members. Write the topic and the sections on the chalkboard.

2. Explain, "Today we'll be learning in a slightly different way. It's called 'Bring Me Your Brains,' and here's how it works: We'll be learning the material in [two, three, or four] sections. You're responsible for knowing the information in each section well enough to present it to the entire class. Look at the board. You'll find today's topic and the sections I will teach it in. As a team, generate a list of at least five questions about this topic. You have three minutes. Begin."

3. After three minutes, continue: "Here's how the rest of the activity works. Rather than teach the whole class, I'll be instructing just one member of your team. That person, in turn, will teach you what he or she learned. While the person is up here with me, you are to be quietly answering the questions based on your team's collective knowledge. Think of an intelligent answer for each one!"

4. Have each team designate a "Brain" to come forward and learn the information from you. Then call out "Bring me

your Brains." While the group of Brains listens to you and takes notes, the remaining team members answer their questions quietly.

5. When the Brains are ready to return to their teams, say: "Teams! Here come your Brains! Please learn well from them. You'll want your notes to be as good as or even better than those of your Brain." Give the Brains just enough time to share their information.

6. Give a brief oral pop quiz, randomly selecting one person from each team to answer a question about that section.

7. Have each team choose a new Brain, and repeat steps 4 to 6. After all the sections have been taught, have each team prepare and deliver a presentation to the class about the information.

❝ I develop thinking skills, teamwork, and communication skills with Bring Me Your Brains. ❞

Making It Mine

For what portion of an upcoming lesson would Bring Me Your Brains be a good fit? Make a note in your planner.

Planned lesson: _____

_____

As you think through this activity, anticipate moments of confusion or lack of focus. Prepare what you will say or do beforehand.

Possible Trouble Spots	What Will I Do?
_____	_____
_____	_____
_____	_____

Reach for the Stars!

Use the stars below to monitor your progress.

I have this tip
down cold!

It is familiar
territory.

This tip feels like a
new pair of shoes.

If a parent asked you about Bring Me Your Brains, what would you say? Write your answer here, or if you prefer, draw an icon that represents this HotTip.

Thinking It Over

What worked well, and how do I know
it worked?

_____

_____

_____

_____

_____

_____

_____

How could I restructure the teams or the process to make this
HotTip more effective?

_____

_____

_____

_____

_____

_____

What do my students say about Bring Me Your Brains?

_____

_____

_____

_____

_____

_____

On a scale of 1 to 10, my students give Bring Me Your Brains a

_____.

Celebrate Success!

Plan momentary celebrations to acknowledge accomplishment and increase motivation to succeed.

Ah! The sweet, sweet smell of success! The road to success is paved with potholes, detours, and speed bumps, but the hardships are what make success smell so sweet and celebration feel so good.

Learning is by nature a risky business that is often met with first-attempt failures. To learn, we must step outside what is comfortable, explore new information that may challenge our preconceived notions, and try on unfamiliar ways. We stumble and bumble until we master the information. And because learning requires all of who we are—our mind, body, and emotions—all of who we are is on the line. Therefore, mastery deserves a party!

Infusing the path of learning with celebrations opens the emotions and increases receptivity to new and greater challenges (Goleman 2000). Celebrations may be as simple and quick or as elaborate as you choose. Either way, they signify accomplishment and build confidence.

There are many ways to celebrate. Here are a few you might want to have students do:

➤ High five your neighbor.
➤ Put a star next to the first step of your math problem.
➤ Write, "Yahoo!" "Excellent!" "Way to go!" on your paper.

- Stand up and do an "end zone" dance.
- Pat yourself on the back and say, "Well done!"
- Smile.
- Say to yourself, "I knew I could do it."
- Take a lap around the class as classmates stand, applaud, and give high tens.

  Celebrations encourage, acknowledge, and increase confidence and competence.

Making It Mine

How often could you and your class celebrate small successes? Take a moment and think of three times during your next class period when everyone could celebrate—even if for no other reason than showing up at school (or class) on time! Choose an appropriate expression of celebration for each.

Time	**Celebration**
1. _____	_____
2. _____	_____
3. _____	_____

You might find it useful to explain to students your desire to infuse more celebration into their learning. Ask them to suggest brief, meaningful celebrations. Be sure to incorporate them into your growing bag of Celebrate Success strategies.

Reach for the Stars!

Use the stars below to monitor your progress.

I have this tip
down cold!

It is familiar
territory.

This tip feels like a
new pair of shoes.

If a school administrator asked you about Celebrate Success, what would you say? Write your answer here, or if you prefer, draw an icon that represents this HotTip.

HotTips for Teachers ©2002 Zephyr Press, Chicago, IL • (800) 232-2187 • www.zephyrpress.com

Thinking It Over

What changes have I noticed since
implementing Celebrate Success?

_____

_____

_____

_____

_____

_____

_____

What are three new ways I could Celebrate Success? (If you need
help, ask a student!)

1. _____

2. _____

3. _____

When I Celebrate Success, I am reminded that students . . .

_____

_____

_____

_____

What difference has Celebrate Success made to my students?

_____

_____

_____

_____

On a scale of 1 to 10, my students give Celebrate Success a _____.

Part 3

HotTips for Closing the Lesson or Unit

Now that your students are used to being fully engaged at the beginning and throughout the lesson, go ahead and dial up the engagement toward the end. Remember your goal: for every student to learn in every lesson, every day. Let them Interview the Expert just before you Pop the Quickie Quiz, then be sure they hand you their Ticket out the Door to show you and themselves that they really did learn something that day. Then, after the students leave, Go Walkabout to enjoy some reflective time with your colleagues. In the process, you will highlight the strengths and improvements in your teaching.

In this section, we talk about accountability. What do we mean by that? We mean being someone others can count on—and it applies to your students as much as to you. Although they will never say it out loud, every day your students come into class asking, "Teacher, what are you going to expect from me today? Can I count on you to challenge me to learn what I need to know? To create a safe place for me to learn? To create an engaging environment where I make choices to learn rather than mark time? To make sure I learned something today?" You are not responsible for students' attitudes or the difficulties they face inside and outside the classroom. But you are accountable for making your class worth students' time. And they are accountable for demonstrating that they rose to your expectations.

Interview the Expert

Have pairs of students role-play being the expert on a topic and a reporter interviewing the expert to review content in an interactive format.

Here is a fun, interactive way for students to review while boosting their confidence. Interview the Expert sessions provide each student with the opportunity to be an expert, the resident know-it-all about the topic being studied: molecular structures, primary colors, counting by 2s, solving for x, analyzing characters—just about anything you deem important for students to master. A partner, acting as an ace reporter hot on the scoop of an exclusive story, interviews each expert.

Here is the procedure:

1. Prior to the Interview the Expert session, have students prepare questions for a world-renowned expert in the topic of study. For example, questions about English parts of speech might include, "What is the difference between a noun and a verb?" "Name as many prepositions as you can." "In your opinion, which is more valuable: an adjective or an adverb?" The only rule is that the question must be drawn from content studied in class or homework.

2. Explain the two roles students will play: expert and interviewer.

> ➤ The experts must stand tall and appear confident and full of knowledge, as if they really are the most prominent experts on the subject. Encourage them to answer questions from memory as much as they can, using their notes only if necessary.

> ➤ Remind the interviewers that they are interviewing the foremost expert on the subject. They are to be polite, allowing the expert time to answer each question, and are to ask prompting questions if necessary. Their job is to make the expert look good in front of the thousands of home viewers glued to their televisions.

3. Divide students into pairs.

4. Let each pair decide who will be the expert and who will be the interviewer, then conduct their interviews.

 I build my students' confidence and competence by using Interview the Expert.

Making It Mine

You may want to take on the expert role during one of your upcoming lessons. Beforehand, help students create questions that elicit from you the pertinent information. Play up your role by wearing appropriate clothing, donning an accent, or carrying a prop. When students ask questions, have them stand, state their affiliation (*The Daily Globe, The Royal Tribune,* and so on), and begin their questions with a phrase such as, "Is it not true that . . . ?" "How would you respond to. . . ?" "In your opinion . . . ?"

Reach for the Stars!

Use the stars below to monitor your progress.

I have this tip down cold!

It is familiar territory.

This tip feels like a new pair of shoes.

If a reporter asked you about Interview the Expert, what would you say? Write your answer here, or if you prefer, draw an icon that represents this HotTip.

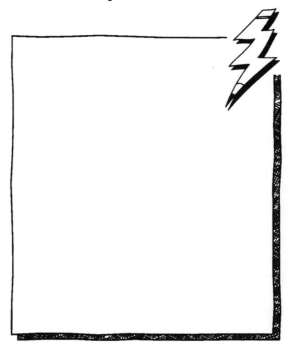

Thinking It Over

What aspects of Interview the Expert
worked well, and how could I tell?

_____

_____

_____

_____

_____

_____

What will I do differently next time?

_____

_____

_____

_____

When I use Interview the Expert, I am reminded that students . . .

_____

_____

_____

_____

What do my students say about Interview the Expert?

_____

_____

_____

_____

On a scale of 1 to 10, my students give Interview the Expert a

_____.

Pop the
Quickie Quiz

Use a short pop quiz to gain feedback
about students' learning and send a
message that they are accountable for
understanding the lesson.

"Class, please clear your
desks for a pop quiz."

A h, those infamous words. Just the sound of them sends a
familiar quiver down most students' spines. ("Ready or not,
here it comes" would be a more accurate statement!) As if the
surprise of an unannounced quiz were not enough, the teacher
would continue with, "You are responsible for everything we cover
in this class. If you are not prepared for this quiz, perhaps in the
future you will use your study time more appropriately." Oh, the
sting of guilt mixed with the shock of a quiz!

The teacher certainly got everyone's attention! With just two little
words, "pop quiz," one person was able to capture the focus of an
entire class. What power! What authority! What brilliance!
Although the motive behind a pop quiz might be questionable at
times, springing the surprise is a stroke of genius.

There is something compelling about an impending event. It kick-starts the mind, throws it into hyperdrive, and sends blood rushing to the brain. In her explanation of motivation theory, Madeline Hunter (1983) referred to this phenomenon as "increasing the level of concern." Similar to Collect a Ticket out the Door (page 138) a quickie quiz heightens students' awareness of the importance of class time while giving you a way to check for understanding.

A quickie quiz contains four questions, problems, or statements directly related to the lesson. It is quick to create and even quicker to grade. To pass, a student must score 75 percent or better. In today's world of standards and high expectations, individual accountability is the name of the game. For every lesson, all students must understand what they learned and be able to demonstrate it.

> ❝ When I Pop a Quickie Quiz, I gain feedback regarding my students' learning. ❞

Making It Mine

Your goal with this strategy is to gain instant feedback about whether students understood what they learned. Ask students to grab a scrap piece of paper. Encourage them to do their best work and to do it solo. Show the questions on the overhead and say them out loud. Move quickly, giving most students time to answer but not waiting for the stragglers. After the fourth question, have students exchange papers and grade each other if appropriate. Make note of who received 100% and who did not. At this point you can meet with those who still need help or assign students from the 100% group to peer tutor the others. Collect all papers so you can see the results firsthand and set the course for your next lesson.

Reach for the Stars!

Use the stars below to monitor your progress.

I have this tip down cold!

It is familiar territory.

This tip feels like a new pair of shoes.

If a colleague asked you about Pop the Quickie Quiz, what would you say? Write your answer here, or if you prefer, draw an icon that represents this HotTip.

Thinking It Over

What aspects of the quickie quiz are
most effective, and how could I tell?

_____

_____

_____

_____

What challenges have I faced with Pop the Quickie Quiz? How
can I resolve those challenges?

Challenge   **Solution**

_____   _____

_____   _____

_____   _____

_____   _____

When I Pop the Quickie Quiz, I am reminded that students . . .

_____

_____

_____

_____

What differences do I see in my students since Popping Quickie
Quizzes?

_____

_____

_____

_____

On a scale of 1 to 10, my students give Pop the Quickie Quiz a

_____.

Collect a Ticket out the Door

Require each student to answer a question about key content of the lesson before leaving class.

You know you taught the content. The students seemed to be with you. A few peeks at their work indicate that students understood the information. But how do you know whether the students really got it? This HotTip increases student accountability during class and increases their sense of responsibility for learning.

Inform students that their "ticket out the door" for the day is the answer(s) to a particular question, set of questions, or mathematical computation. You might present it this way:

> "I saw great focus and participation during the lesson today. You're probably feeling confident about what you learned, and so you should be! Let's be sure we've really got it by playing 'ticket out the door.' Here's how it works. Your answer to a particular question is your 'ticket' or permission to leave class. If you have your ticket, you leave. If you don't, we hang out together until you understand the answer. Today's ticket out the door is the answer to this question: 'Name the stages of the water cycle.' Please stand if you know the answer. Get help with the answer if you need it."

You may either elicit an answer from each student individually, dismissing students one at a time, or let one person answer for the row or table group. Mix up the requirements or even the question to extend students' thinking. For example, "Name the stage that rain would be in (pause) Robert," or "Name one thing besides the water cycle we've learned this year (pause) Cindy." Since you have a limited number of questions, you will ask the same question to more than one student, reinforcing key content and giving students an incentive to listen carefully so they know the answer when their turn comes.

Holding students accountable for what transpired in class serves three purposes: (1) It communicates the importance of participation; (2) it sends a message that you expect students to learn what you taught, and (3) it increases students' sense of competence as they master the content.

 When I Collect a Ticket out the Door, I know for sure my students understood the **lesson.**

Making It Mine

What will be your students' ticket out the door for your next lesson? What is the most important idea, concept, or bit of knowledge you want your students to walk away with? A math fact? A part of speech? A formula? As students answer, remember to acknowledge them with a high five, accolade, or simple "thank you."

Reach for the Stars!

Use the stars below to monitor your progress.

I have this tip
down cold!

It is familiar
territory.

This tip feels like a
new pair of shoes.

If a colleague asked you about Collect a Ticket out the Door, what would you say? Write your answer here, or if you prefer, draw an icon that represents this HotTip.

Thinking It Over

What benefits have I noticed from this
HotTip?

_____

_____

_____

_____

_____

What will I do differently next time?

_____

_____

_____

When I Collect a Ticket out the Door, I am reminded that students . . .

_____

_____

_____

What do my students say about Collect a Ticket out the Door?

_____

_____

_____

What differences have I noticed in students' learning since I have
Collected Tickets out the Door?

_____

_____

_____

Go Walkabout

Use this self-coaching strategy to analyze and debrief after a lesson, preferably with a few colleagues.

As we navigate the waters of educational innovation, we are faced with challenges: How do we design and facilitate sensory-rich, challenging experiences for our students? How do we assist students to take greater responsibility for their learning and at the same time meet or exceed standards? How do we accelerate understanding and retention while fostering transfer? These are big questions that require us to consider what we do, how we do it, and how what we do affects our students.

This HotTip is a self-coaching process in which you ask yourself provocative questions that improve and accelerate your ability to create quality educational experiences. Although this process can be completed individually, it is far more powerful in trios, so enlist a couple of supportive colleagues and go for it!

The Overview

One person at a time completes the activity by answering six questions. The other two people listen and observe, watching for nonverbal changes in posture, gesture, voice, tone, tempo, and volume as they carefully witness their colleague's walkabout.

The Process

1. Choose six different locations in your room. This is the walkabout path. You will answer one question in each location.

2. Think back on a lesson you designed and delivered to your students.

3. With the lesson in mind, answer the six questions listed on the next page as you move around the walkabout path.

4. Debrief in an area away from the six walkabout locations.

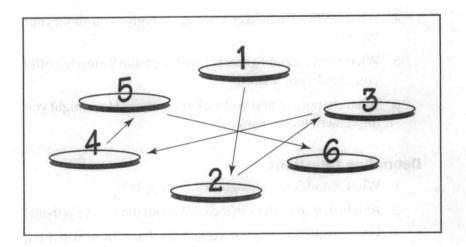

 By continually striving to improve, I give my students a model for being the best they can be.

Making It Mine

Use the following questions in the self-analysis process:

Walkabout Questions

1. What was your outcome?

2. As a result of the lesson, what did you hope would be different in your students' lives?

3. What feedback would supportive students give you about the strengths of your lesson?

4. What feedback would critical students give you about your lesson?

5. What advice would a coach, mentor, or master teacher offer you about your lesson?

6. What changes would you make next time? How might you implement those changes?

Debriefing Questions

1. What reminders or insights did you gain?

2. At which step or steps in the walkabout did you gain them?

3. What feedback do your colleagues have from watching your walkabout?

Reach for the Stars!

Use the stars below to monitor your progress.

I have this tip
down cold!

It is familiar
territory.

This tip feels like a
new pair of shoes.

If a colleague asked you about Go Walkabout, what would you say? Write your answer here, or if you prefer, draw an icon that represents this HotTip.

Thinking It Over

What are my strengths as a teacher?

_____

_____

_____

_____

_____

_____

What is the one thing I would most like to improve about my teaching?

_____

_____

_____

_____

_____

_____

What other questions would I like to use in future walkabouts?

1. _____

2. _____

3. _____

4. _____

5. _____

6. _____

> **All students are gifted— some just open their packages earlier than others.**
>
> —Michael Carr

Further Learning

Abernathy, Rob, and Mark Reardon. 2002. *HotTips for Speakers: 25 Surefire Ways to Engage and Captivate Any Group or Audience.* Tucson, Ariz.: Zephyr Press.

Armstrong, Thomas. 1993. *Seven Kinds of Smart.* New York: Penguin Books.

Bandler, Richard. 1985. *Using Your Brain—For a Change.* Moab, UT: Real People Press.

Caine, Renate N., and Geoffrey Caine. 1994. *Making Connections: Teaching and the Human Brain.* Menlo Park, Calif.: Addison-Wesley.

——. 1997. *Education on the Edge of Possibility.* Alexandria, Va.: Association of Supervision and Curriculum Development.

Campbell, Don G. 1992. *100 Ways to Improve Your Teaching Using Your Voice and Music: Pathways to Accelerate Learning.* Tucson, Ariz.: Zephyr Press.

DePorter, Bobbi. 1992. *Quantum Learning.* New York: Dell.

DePorter, Bobbi, Sarah Singer-Nourie, and Mark Reardon. 1999. *Quantum Teaching: Orchestrating Student Success.* Needham Heights, Mass.: Allyn & Bacon.

Gardner, Howard. 1993. *Frames of Mind.* New York: Basic Books.

Goleman, Daniel. 1997. *Emotional Intelligence.* New York: Bantam Books.

——. 2000. *Working with Emotional Intelligence.* New York: Bantam Books.

Harmin, Merrill. 1995. *Inspiring Active Learning.* Edwardsville, Ill.: Inspiring Strategies Institute.

Hart, Leslie. 1983. *Human Brain, Human Learning.* New York: Brain Age Publishers.

Hunter, Madeline. 1983. *Motivation Theory.* El Segundo, Calif.: TIP Publications.

Jensen, Eric. 1994. *The Learning Brain.* Del Mar, Calif.: Turning Point.

————. 1995. *Brain-Based Learning and Teaching.* Del Mar, Calif.: Turning Point.

Kagan, Spencer, and Miguel Kagan. 1998. *Multiple Intelligences: The Complete MI Book.* San Clemente, Calif.: Kagan Cooperative Learning.

Lazear, David. 2000. *Pathways of Learning: Teaching Students and Parents about Multiple Intelligences.* Tucson, Ariz.: Zephyr Press.

Rose, Colin, and M. J. Nicholl. 1998. *Accelerated Learning for the Twenty-First Century.* New York: Delacorte Press.

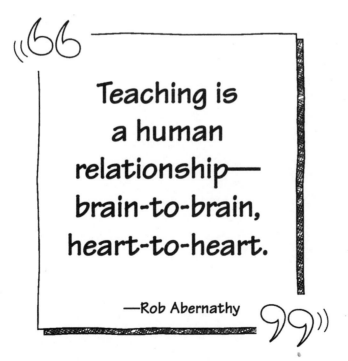

Teaching is
a human
relationship—
brain-to-brain,
heart-to-heart.

—Rob Abernathy

About the Authors

Rob Abernathy is recognized as among the top trainers in the United States. Currently CEO of Intertrainment, a consulting firm that sponsors seminars on curriculum development, accountability in education, and assessment issues, Abernathy previously worked for the Orange County Department of Education and the Orange County California School Leadership Academy facilitating a variety of training experiences for educators. He holds a master's degree in educational administration from Azuza Pacific University, as well as administrative, special education, and multiple-subject teaching credentials. He is coauthor of the *HotTips* series.

Mark Reardon is president of Centre Pointe Education, culminating twenty-one years of experience as a teacher, principal, and educational consultant. Throughout his career, his focus has remained on discovering what works in teaching and learning. Drawing on his bachelor's in psychology from California Lutheran University and his master's in educational administration from California State University, Fullerton, Reardon translates learning theory into understandable, usable practices for educators. He has taught learners of all ages, from children to university professors, parents to CEOs. His expertise encompasses professional development, train-the-trainer seminars, communication and team-building skills, as well as curriculum and program design. He is coauthor of *Quantum Teaching: Orchestrating Student Success* and the *HotTips* series.